D0481518

The Microwave Oven Cookbook

OTHER BOOKS BY LOYTA WOODING
The Cooking Collectarium
Smart Shopper's Cookbook
Meals on Wheels

The Microwave Oven Cookbook

Loyta Wooding

**Designed and Illustrated
by Kadi Karist Tint**

Nash Publishing, Los Angeles

Diagrams in
"What You Should Know About Microwave Cooking"
by Raymond E. Higgins

Copyright © 1972 by Loyta Wooding

All rights reserved. No part of this book
may be reproduced in any form or by any means
without permission in writing from the publisher.

Library of Congress Catalog Card Number: 79-186922
Standard Book Number: 8402-1265-8

Published simultaneously in the United States and
Canada by Nash Publishing Corporation,
9255 Sunset Boulevard, Los Angeles, California 90069.

Printed in the United States of America.

Eighth Printing

For Sir Reginald and Lady Sholl
Melbourne, Australia

Contents

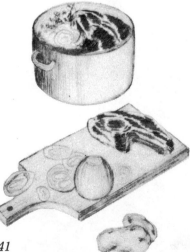

Foreword

Microwave cooking is the answer to every homemaker's dream. This dramatic innovation will revolutionize conventional cooking ideas, streamline kitchens and change eating habits to an unbelievable degree.

Even now, in its infancy, microwave cooking gives a much-needed helping hand to the busy women of today's world. As more and more homemakers become involved in many activities away from home, the microwave oven makes it possible for them to feed their families without feeling guiltily that they are neglecting their domestic responsibilities; they are able to prepare satisfying meals without worrying that they are short-changing their families nutritionally.

There are so many other advantages, too. No more overcooked dinners while waiting for the family to come home. With a microwave oven a homemaker can wait until she sees them coming, and cook dinner while they wash up. When someone is not home at mealtime, she will be

able to store the food in the refrigerator and reheat it in one minute right in the serving plate.

And as for entertaining, the entire food preparation concept is undergoing a change. She can prepare food ahead of time, put it in the serving dishes and, at mealtime, heat it in the microwave oven in minutes and serve it at the table or the buffet.

The modern homemaker will be ever ready to receive unannounced visitors. In most homes there is always some food in the freezer. But how long does it take to defrost it without a microwave oven? Now meats, vegetables, and desserts can be thawed and cooked in minutes.

For short orders, it is invaluable. Imagine heating a hot dog and bun in twenty-five seconds, and a bowl of soup in one minute.

Microwave cooking is so different that, at first, it startles everyone. It's fun to watch a cake rise right before your eyes, make a sauce without continually stirring, or roast a majestic turkey in thirty minutes.

With all these extraordinary advantages one wonders why the microwave-cooking concept has taken so long to develop. Although microwave ovens have been around for a number of years, they are only now coming into their own as appliances for home use. The developmental cycle is no different from that of television, if one recalls the delays of the general public in accepting TV. Another factor in the slow development of the microwave oven is that, at the moment, their designs and prices are in the deluxe range, but a few years from now they will be commonplace as supplements to today's standard electric and gas ranges, and, in the not far-off future, they will be alternatives to our present-day ranges.

The microwave oven, in one form or another, will be as common an appliance in the home and apartment as the air-conditioner and garbage disposal. Its growth in sales will undoubtedly parallel the growth of television and, before that, the freezer.

I can crystal-gaze now and predict that food preparation, in the traditional sense, will eventually disappear from the home scene as a result of microwave cooking. In support of this is the impressive fact that one meal in four is now eaten singly, and not at a family gathering. In a few years it may well be one meal in three and, beyond that, who knows? And my further prediction is that the concept of kitchenless houses and apartments is not too far off—that is, based on microwave-oven heating and freezer storage only.

For those swinging singles and childless couples, apartment buildings will have frozen-food vending machines right in the lobby, from which the working couple or person will be able to purchase their food requirements according to their individual choice; where, in minutes, a hot, tasty, attractive, and nourishing meal will be prepared in their microwave oven with after-meal cleanup involving little more than dropping the empty containers and disposable utensils down the incinerator chute.

There are about twenty available brands of microwave ovens to choose from, with more on the way. This book is an attempt to fulfill a need of the average homemaker to understand this new basic principle in cooking and how best to utilize it.

LOYTA WOODING

The Microwave Oven Cookbook

What You Should Know About Microwave Cooking

Before you proceed with the actual menu planning and cooking of foods by microwave energy, you should have a firm understanding of what exactly it is, how it can fit into your kitchen routine to save labor and help prepare food more efficiently. Your questions must be answered to your satisfaction because, after all, in the end you must decide whether or not to buy a microwave oven.

So let's start at the very beginning and take you, step by step, through the entire process and show you just what a microwave oven is supposed to do in your home.

1. What Is Microwave Energy?

You probably have heard a lot about microwave energy, but do you really know what it is?

Microwave energy consists of waves which we cannot see, but of whose existence we know because we are able to

observe their effect. The process of emitting energy in the form of waves is known as *radiation*, the name given to the energy waves collectively. These waves radiate outward from the center just as when you throw a pebble on a quiet surface of water and waves are formed which move outward from the point where the pebble first broke the surface of the water, forming one circle after another as they widen.

Of course, the radiation waves travel much faster. They travel at the speed of light, 186,283 miles per second and carry bunches of energy which are called *photons* and which vibrate at various frequencies.

You are probably familiar with the frequencies in radio and television so that you know that a frequency is the number of complete cycles of current produced by an alternating-current generator per second. Thus, a frequency of 25,000 cycles per second means that there is an alternator generating a complete wave (a cycle) 25,000 times each second.

All electromagnetic waves—radio and light waves—can be described by their wavelengths and their frequencies, and they may be broken down as follows:

Nonionizing

Used for radio broadcasting:
    Long wave
    Medium wave
    Short wave

Used for radio telephone:
    Ultrashort wave

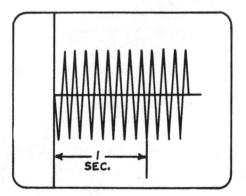

4

The heat from the sun, electric fires, etc., is :
    Infrared

For medical apparatus and cooking:
    Microwave

Ionizing

These are visible lights and can cause chemical changes without any significant temperature rise:
    Gamma rays
    Cosmic rays
    Ultraviolet rays

Radiant or electromagnetic waves are characterized by their wavelength and their frequency of vibration, the number of complete cycles per second, so that when you combine wavelength and frequency the result is the speed of light. When a radio wave of a specific wavelength is transmitted from an aerial, it can be picked up by a receiving aerial, reconverted into electric currents which intermit at the transmission frequency.

Microwaves vibrate millions of times per second. In other words, they have a very high frequency and are therefore very short waves; this is the reason they are called "microwaves."

Microwaves are waves whose wavelengths lie between those of ultrashort radio waves and infrared waves. And like all radio and light waves, they may be absorbed, reflected, or transmitted.

2. Who Controls the Use of Microwave Energy?

The United States Federal Communications Commission, popularly known as the FCC, controls and allocates the frequencies for industrial, scientific, and medical uses, and sees to it that a frequency assigned to one is not taken over by another. All radio and television stations are licensed for uses as specified by the FCC. Since the oven emits electromagnetic waves somewhat like a broadcasting station, if you purchase or now own a microwave oven, you will be required to be registered as the owner with the manufacturer, so that the location of the oven will be known at all times. If you sell it, or purchase one through an original owner, you are required to notify the manufacturer.

The FCC has allocated two microwave frequencies for use by microwave ovens which are identified by the symbol MHz, meaning "megahertz," the term describing the millions of cycles per second. "Mega" is derived from a Greek word signifying "great, large, powerful," as in "megalopolis." It has come to mean "a million, multiplied by a million." "Hertz" is taken from the name

5

of Heinrich Hertz, the German physicist who first detected electromagnetic waves and later succeeded in producing them.

The two microwave frequencies are:

915 MHz

2450 MHz

This means that a microwave frequency at 915 MHz has a wavelength of about 12.5 inches, and the 2450 MHz has a wavelength of about 5 inches.

So then, microwave energy is energy vibrating at microwave frequencies and moving at the speed of light. The effect of the microwaves on food (or other material) placed in the path of this energy, once it becomes absorbed, is that it produces a rise in temperature.

In a microwave oven, the electromagnetic waves are produced by a magnetron. In other words, the waves are connected to the oven cavity in which the food is placed and the food is exposed to the electromagnetic waves that cause it to become hot quickly because it has absorbed energy from the microwaves.

This energy is transferred into heat within the substance itself and, since substances are composed of different cellular combinations, they tend to absorb the microwaves differently; thus, the heating rate is influenced by the composition of each food in regard to mass, weight, and shape. For example, a white cream sauce is a mass of food of a fairly even construction and it would be easy to heat. But a rib roast of beef, consisting of lean meat, fat, gristle, and sometimes bone, would be more difficult to heat at a uniform rate.

Therefore the consistency of the food to be heated is an important factor which influences the speed at which it is cooked.

3. Can All Materials Be Heated by Microwave Energy?

All matter is made up of atoms and molecules. But some of the molecules of some materials are electrically neutral, that is, they have no electrical charge and microwave energy can pass through them as if they were not there. Matter which is not electrically neutral is converted to heat when the microwave energy is applied.

A microwave oven cooks by means of dielectric (nonconducting) loss: this means that food materials, being essentially poor electrical conductors (dielectrics), take energy from the microwaves and convert it to heat; that is, the microwaves lose energy to the food. These microwaves penetrate deeply into the food material giving up energy as they penetrate. This energy causes the molecules of the food to vibrate 2,450 million times each second, thus creating a sort of intermolecular friction which results in heat and accomplishes the cooking action.

6

Like the light waves, microwave energy is reflected. Metals reflect microwaves and the waves will not penetrate them, nor can they transmit heat. For this reason, utensils used in cooking the food in conventional gas or electric ovens or on top of the range, made of metal or aluminum foil, are not suitable for microwave cooking (although aluminum foil is occasionally used as explained on pages 11 and 18). However, as manufacturers change and improve the ovens, metal utensils will become usable.

There are other materials which can transmit microwaves to the food because they do not reflect and, therefore, the energy passes through them since there is no absorption. It is as if they were not there. To make this point clearer, let us assume that on a cold sunny day you are sitting in your car, facing the sun. You have not turned on the car heater, but you do feel warm and comfortable because the sun's rays are passing through the glass window, without heating it but reaching you. If you touch the window it will be cold. However, the molecules in your body are electrically charged and are converting the sun's energy to heat, and so you feel warm.

This is the reason that shopkeepers are forced to shade their display windows when the sun is strong, as the sun's rays can penetrate the glass causing bacteriological change in foods and fading materials.

The nonconductive materials are known as dielectric materials and, besides glass, they may be paper, plastics, china, etc., items which cannot be used in conventional cooking methods, except perhaps for glass or china if it is ovenproof.

The nonconductive material, in other words, is material through which the force of an electrostatic field will pass to reach the material (food) which has molecules and may be heated.

4. What Is a Microwave Oven?

A microwave oven is an oven constructed of metal so that the walls of the cavity can reflect microwaves in many paths within the cavity. It has a door, the magnetron, a waveguide, a mode stirrer, power supply, power cord, and controls.

The main function of the power supply is to convert low voltage-line power to the high voltages required by the microwave-energy generator, the magnetron. When the magnetron is energized it generates high-frequency energy which then passes down the waveguide to the cavity. The mode stirrer, as it turns, interrupts the energy as it enters the cavity and causes it to be distributed all over the inside of the cavity before it is absorbed by the food. Without the mode stirrer, only straight waves would enter the cavity, and the food would not be cooked evenly.

7

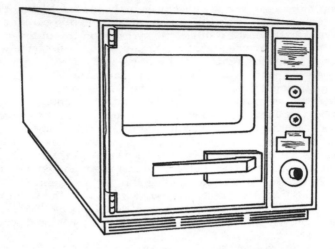

The food is placed off the floor of the oven so that the energy is also reflected from the oven floor into the food from below. If this were not done the bottom of the food would lag behind in cooking, making the food unevenly done.

The important characteristic of the microwaves is that they penetrate deeply into the food and produce heat immediately, as they penetrate, so that we are able to heat or cook foods in an oven on utensils which will be cool to the touch, and may often be removed from the oven without pot holders. Sometimes, however, the utensils become warm or hot, taking heat from the food itself.

The oven controls consist of: a timer, indicating lights, a start or cook button, and a master switch. Timers vary from one manufacturer to the next, but they are reasonably accurate, and are usually marked so that very short heating cycles can be set. The timer is important because all microwave cooking is gauged by time, not temperature-and-time as in conventional cooking.

A few minutes excess time in conventional cooking is not catastrophic, but it is in a microwave oven where every second counts. Therefore, be sure to study the manufacturer's manual giving the exact times required for heating and cooking in your particular microwave oven model and follow *this* cookbook only as a guideline and inspiration for recipes.

An audio signal indicates when the set time has elapsed and the oven has turned itself off. The oven may also be turned off simply by opening the door. This protects the user from unnecessary exposure to microwave energy, as three interlocks operate when the door is opened and any one of them turns off the oven. The oven can also be turned off by turning the timer back to zero time or by turning off the master switch.

8

In some models the cook button is omitted, and cooking action is initiated simply by closing the door. In such ovens, a thick glass shelf provides the required suitable load in the event that the door is inadvertently closed with time still remaining on the timer, because an empty cavity with the energy still on, will cause damage to the interior.

Microwave ovens require either 115 or 220 volts depending on the model. In most cases they will present no strain on available power.

The most popular type of microwave oven is a portable counter-top unit for microwave cooking only. It operates on 115 volts and does not require special wiring, but the circuit should not be overloaded by the addition of other appliances.

5. What About Servicing the Microwave Oven?

Most manufacturers provide service on a nationwide basis. Generally, ovens are guaranteed for one to two years from the date of purchase for replacement or repair of parts found to be

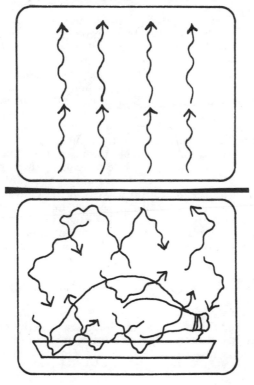

defective as to workmanship or material under normal use, including labor.

Warranty on the magnetron, which is the power source which generates the microwave energy, may be one or two years depending on the manufacturer, paralleling the warranty of the picture tube for a television set. Under normal usage, the magnetron will usually last for several thousand actual cooking hours.

6. Are All Microwave Ovens Alike?

No, they are not. The most popular oven has a power of 1000 watts (1 kilowatt). To properly develop a sense of timing in microwave cooking, it is first necessary to know how much power is available in your oven.

The waves, or energy distribution, in the cavity depend on the skill of the manufacturer in matching the dimensions of the oven cavity to the electromagnetic field transmitted from the magnetron. This means that the distribution of the microwaves should be as even as possible to achieve consistent heating which will give best cooking results.

In conventional cooking this depends on the conduction of heat from the food surface to the inside and it can only be accelerated by increasing the oven temperature. But in microwave cooking the microwaves pass into the surface layers and heat is generated. Those waves not absorbed by the surface layers are transmitted to the next layer, and then to the next one of the food mass. The waves are reflected in many paths throughout the oven cavity and they penetrate the food from all directions, converting into heat. In other words, the food is cooked not by applying heat to the surface but by generating it within the food itself.

When the food is removed from the microwave oven, the heat distribution still continues at a rate dependent upon the thermal conductivity of the food, so that food cooked by microwave remains hotter longer than food cooked in the conventional way.

If we were to place a metallic substance in the microwave oven cavity, the even pattern would be distorted since the walls of the oven are proportioned to match the performance of the magnetron and this would result in food unevenly heated or cooked.

7. Do All Foods Cook at the Same Rate?

No, they do not. First, moisture plays an important role. Most foods contain moisture in varying amounts with the exception of fats or dehydrated foods. The amount of moisture in a food will have a direct bearing on its heating rate. One pound of food with 30 percent moisture will take less time to heat to a specific

10

temperature than one pound of food with 50 percent moisture. Or, if both foods are placed in the oven cavity at the same time, the former will cook faster than the latter.

The temperature of the food is also important. When two foods at different starting temperatures, one refrigerated, the other at room temperature, are placed in the oven simultaneously, the colder food will take longer to heat than the warmer food. The manufacturer's cooking instructions, when giving heating or cooking time, will also designate the temperature of the food to be cooked or heated.

8. Which Foods Should Be Cooked by Microwave?

Heating and cooking food by microwave energy gives superior results for many foods. Foods that are canned, bottled liquids, and bakery products are very quickly heated. Poaching, baking, and steaming by cooking the individual product by microwave alone, produce superior dishes.

White meats, poultry, and fish are fine when cooked from the raw state and using a combination method of microwave and the conventional process. If browning and crisping are required, the cook need merely use the microwave oven as a time accelerator, cooking the product by microwave energy, and then browning it quickly by a conventional broiling method.

The rate at which a product is heated is partially determined by its water content which readily absorbs power at microwave frequency. Thus the high moisture content of fish makes it an ideal product for microwave cooking.

Food with an open, porous texture is easily penetrated by the microwaves. It is easier to heat meat which has been conventionally precooked because the muscle fiber has already received a slow heat application and it has merged with the fat to form a more even mass.

9. Do You Need Special Utensils for Microwave Heating or Cooking?

Generally speaking, you will find it easier to heat or cook food by microwave because serving dishes, glass, china, or crockery may be used.

Manufacturers object to the use of metal. Even small amounts of metal present in the oven will reflect the microwaves so that they will not penetrate the food to be cooked.

There are exceptions with regard to the use of thin aluminum foil. A circle of aluminum foil placed in the center of a slice of leftover roast will keep it from becoming too well done. When

11

heating a casserole, the use of a strip of foil around the edge will slow down the heating effect in this area and insure a hotter center.

Oven-proof and plain glass, ceramics, chinaware, plastic ware, paper containers, plastic film may be used. Some plastics, such as melamine, absorb enough energy to cause charring, and others, such as styrene, give off a strong odor. But most plastic materials offered by food manufacturers are made of polyethylene and polypropylene, which are quite acceptable.

Paper plates and containers should not be wax-coated because the wax absorbs microwave energy, thus melting and transferring the flavor to the food. If you use paper plates, be sure there are no printed patterns or words, and dinnerware or glass cookware with painted designs or metal trims or attachments should not be used because they retard the heating process.

The walls of the microwave oven are metallic and, being proportioned to match the performance of the magnetron, help to produce an electromagnetic pattern of waves that will evenly heat and cook food. If you place another metallic substance in the microwave oven, the even pattern will be distorted and you may see flashes in the cavity. This is known as "arcing." Arcing may also occur if the power of the microwave oven is switched on while the cavity is empty, thus threatening the life of the magnetron.

This also means that a meat thermometer cannot be used in the microwave oven. To test a roast for doneness you may take it out of the oven, insert the thermometer, take the reading, remove the thermometer, and return the roast to the oven if additional cooking time is required.

The removable handles of some glass cookware may be of metal, and a careful check should be made before using glassware.

If arcing should occur, turn off the oven and check the cookware carefully for metal.

If you are in doubt about the use of a particular utensil in the microwave oven, perform this simple test:

Check the utensil for any visible metal parts or trim, and do not use it if any exist.

Fill a heatproof glass cup with water and place the full cup in the utensil that is being checked.

Place in the microwave oven; set the timer for 1¼ minutes.

If the water is warm and the utensil is cool, the result is satisfactory. If the utensil is warm or even hot and the water is still cool or just barely lukewarm, *do not use* the utensil for microwave cooking.

12

Covering some foods when reheating them is recommended. The cover prevents loss of moisture and also keeps foods from drying out. Steam generated from the food is kept in close contact with the food, and in this way helps to provide a more uniformly heated product. Plastic films, punctured in the center to allow some of the steam to escape, make very satisfactory covers.

Precooked frozen foods in plastic pouches may be heated in the package in microwave ovens provided that a few punctures are made in the pouch to relieve the inside pressure.

Most cooking utensils may be removed without pot holders. If dishes get warm it is because heat transfers from the food. Of course, you do add heat when you turn on the browning unit in the microwave oven, and if you are going to cook a food in combination microwave and conventional ovens, then be sure to use oven-proof utensils.

10. How Safe Is a Microwave Oven?

In 1968, Congress passed a Radiation Control for Health and Safety Act known as Public Law 90-602. One of the purposes of this law was to establish standards for allowable amounts of radiation of various electronic products. Not only microwave ovens, but television sets, medical equipment, and sun lamps are covered by this law.

Microwave ovens have improved enormously during the last two years, and doors have become better fitting to avoid radiation leakage. There are instruments available which can easily detect radiation presence since radiation is not visible.

The oven door is very important because not only does it provide access to the cavity, but it also confines the microwave energy. A properly fitted door is essential to completely confine the energy, and the door flange should be wiped clean frequently to insure good contact of the door and the door flange.

A good microwave oven should have a choke seal around the perimeter of the door which acts as a buffer to cancel out microwave emissions. Others have a metal-to-metal contact, but if food should splatter and spill on or between the door and the flange, it would form a pathway for microwave energy leakage, and should not be permitted to accumulate.

Microwave ovens are required to have two safety interlocks on the oven door, at least one of which is inaccessible except to a servicing man. Other interlocks on the cabinet prevent the oven from being operated if the cover has been removed.

If a microwave oven door is noticeably loose, or if the oven door can be opened even slightly before the door interlocks are heard to click, the oven should be checked for leakage.

A quick, simple, and safe test for leakage is to place a cup of

13

cold water in the oven, turn on the timer for 5 seconds, and then run a finger around the edge of the door. If even a slight warmth is felt at any point, it means that the oven is probably leaking.

There is little need for concern, however, about hazards of microwave oven use when one considers the fact that microwave diathermy treatments are carried out by the medical profession at levels of radiation over 100 times greater than the microwave oven radiation.

The microwave oven is equipped with a three-prong (grounding) appliance plug for your protection against possibly hazardous electrical shock.

Under no circumstances should you cut or remove the grounding prong from the appliance-cord plug and, if a two-prong adaptor plug is to be used temporarily, it is your responsibility, not the manufacturer's, to engage the services of a qualified electrician and have the adaptor properly grounded and polarized.

11. What Are the Advantages and Disadvantages of Microwave Heating and Cooking?

Microwave ovens cook electronically and operate on a different principle from that of conventional ovens. In an electric or gas oven food cooks when the air in the oven is heated. In microwave cooking, however, the food is cooked electronically while the air inside the oven stays cool. Pots and pans stay cool as well, until the cooked foods they contain heat them somewhat. Cool cooking makes the microwave oven easy to clean. Simply wipe off the interior with a damp cloth.

Microwaves produced inside the oven cook the food by penetration. Food cooks on the outside and inside at the same time, but not at the same rate of speed because microwaves diminish in strength as they work their way into the food. As the microwaves penetrate foods, a small amount of power is lost to each successive layer of molecules in the food. So food is cooked more on the outside than the inside. This cooking pattern makes it possible to cook a beef roast, rare, medium or well-done.

The microwave oven's biggest appeal is speed. It can capsule hours of cooking time into minutes. It has the ability to reheat precooked food in seconds, and make it taste as if it had been freshly prepared.

It is also invaluable for a variety of other heating chores such as heating soups, beverages, rolls, baby foods, baby bottles, hot towels and hot packs, as well as the rapid thawing of frozen foods.

Electronic cooking offers other time-saving features: Since the walls of the oven do not get hot, food spatterings will not burn on, and the oven is easy to keep clean. Because cooking dishes get

14

their only heat from the hot food, not from the oven, you can use a greater variety of dishes for cooking than you can use normally when cooking in the conventional way. You can bake a dessert, for example, right in the individual serving dishes.

Timing must be reasonably precise, otherwise overheating and consequent dehydration can occur. The microwave oven cooks rapidly and food can overcook easily.

When heating or cooking food in the microwave oven, you have to take into greater consideration the starting condition of the food than you would if you were using the conventional approach. For instance, if you heat a frozen prepackaged meal in a conventional oven, it will take 35 to 45 minutes to reach serving temperature from a frozen state, or 20 to 25 minutes from a refrigerated state. But in a microwave oven it would take 1½ minutes from a frozen state and 45 seconds from a refrigerated state. A timing error of 3 to 5 or even 10 minutes in the conventional oven would not be serious, but an error of 1 or 2 minutes in the microwave oven would be disastrous.

Consideration should, therefore, be given to this changing cooking concept. At first, it may seem like a formidable task, but with a little experience you will remember to do it automatically.

Experience will teach you to judge when foods are done, just as in conventional cooking. You should learn to adjust the time according to the quantity and temperature of food, consulting the manufacturer's instructions and cookbook, bearing in mind always that it is better to undercook and allow for the carry-over cooking which occurs after the food is removed from the oven and the heating process continues for a while.

It is easy to overcook foods in a microwave oven, especially at first. You may think the food is not quite done and add time—and overcook it. It is best to check foods frequently at first. When food cooks this fast, the time difference between "just right" and "overdone" can be amazingly short.

In some of the smaller microwave ovens, foods need more attention during cooking than they would in a conventional oven. Foods need to be turned while cooking, sometimes more than once, so that they will cook evenly; in mixed foods, such as casseroles, the utility pans must be turned around during cooking.

Microwave ovens cannot broil food and do not give the golden crisp finish normally associated with various types of food. Learn to use the microwave oven as a new basic principle in cookery to develop fast-cooking and more varied methods, and consider it as complementary equipment to the other cooking appliances in the kitchen, rather than a competitive one. In this way there will never be any restriction in the menus. You will be able to precook many foods and stock the refrigerator and freezer so that you can be flexible in adjusting your schedule to feed your family when they are hungry. If the family cannot assemble around the dining table at the same time, a microwave oven will prove invaluable.

A microwave oven can be moved from area to area, wherever there is electricity, and your patio and backyard parties can be impromptu affairs and easy to handle no matter how large a crowd you entertain.

A vacation or summer cottage would also be an ideal spot to have a microwave oven, and the same is true if you have a houseboat. You will be able to prepare many foods earlier in the day and refrigerate them, then heat them for 10 or 15 seconds in the microwave oven and have a meal ready in 3 minutes, in less time than it would take you to just heat a skillet over a surface unit. A great variety of sandwiches can be heated in the microwave oven. A roast beef sandwich is much more appetizing served hot. Melted cheese sandwiches are especially good, and even pizza may be heated in the oven.

Of course, lunch is not always a sandwich, but quick, simple meals can be served in minutes or seconds using leftovers or precooked foods from the refrigerator. Leftovers do not have the "warmed over" taste when heated in the microwave oven. And, of course, many of the convenience entrees removed from their aluminum containers, and boil-in-the-bag vegetables can be used to advantage, especially if you have forgotten to take things out of the freezer in time to thaw for meals.

Even drying out bread for bread crumbs can be done in seconds, and shortening, margarine, and butter can be measured more accurately after being softened or melted for a few seconds in the oven.

At breakfast time the microwave oven really excels. As is common with many families, breakfast is an extended affair with husband and children rising, dressing, and departing for work or school at different times. This can be a very trying experience for a homemaker when she serves as the coordinator of all morning activities, including cooking. In the end she may become thoroughly frustrated as the baby wakes up crying for his morning bottle while she is pursuing her teen-agers who decide to leave home without waiting for their breakfast to cook.

With a microwave oven, the baby's bottle is warmed in seconds, and single servings of a hot, nutritious breakfast are ready as soon as each member of the family arrives on the scene. Bacon or sausage may be cooked in a conventional manner, stored in the refrigerator, then served with eggs prepared to order at the time required. Bacon and sausage may also be cooked in the microwave oven in sufficient quantities and set aside.

Since the microwave oven eliminates the necessity of having cooked foods stand at room temperatures for longer periods, as when cooked in the conventional way, it diminishes the possibility of bacteria in foods.

16

12. What Effect Does Microwave Energy Have on the Nutritive Value of Foods?

Generally, the nutritional effect on foods is about the same as in conventional heating methods. When, however, the food-service method being used involves keeping foods warm on steam tables in restaurants or food warmers at home for a period of time, vitamin losses can be significant, and heating in microwave ovens is preferrable from a nutritional standpoint. Then the vitamin retention is impressive.

In many instances, the natural vitamins are retained when vegetables are cooked in a microwave oven because they are often done without the addition of water; thus, there is no loss of vitamins, whereas in the conventional cooking method, vegetables are cooked in water and usually, as studies have shown, the homemaker discards the liquid which contains a good percentage of the vitamins.

Important Points to Remember

Starting Temperature. The higher the starting temperature, the faster the food will be heated or cooked. For best results, frozen food should be placed in the microwave oven for a short time so that the surface layers will become warm, then the food should be withdrawn and allowed to stand for five minutes in order that the heat may flow from the hotter region to the cold center. The food may then be returned to the microwave oven and heated for the normal amount of time that the manufacturer gives in the chart for food heated directly from a refrigerated state.

In other words, the microwave oven is used first as a defroster, then as a cooking medium, but one must learn not to use the microwave oven only as a defroster.

Consistency. The denser the food, the longer it will take to heat. A fairly small but thick piece of steak may be similar in size to a hamburger but the steak consists of a diverse formation of fat, gristle, lean meat, and marbled meat, and it will take longer to cook in a microwave oven. I would like to suggest that the steak be seared or broiled first to give it color. This may also be done after it has been cooked in the microwave oven, if desired.

When heating a fairly deep, dense mass of food such as a pie, the center of the food will always be the coolest part and the most difficult to heat. Making a well or inserting a rolled-up one-inch brown paper in the center will cause the air space to transmit microwave energy to the center. A similar effect may be achieved by inserting wooden picks here and there and removing them after the cooking is completed.

17

Making impressions on food surfaces, or indentations, helps speed up the generation of heat.

Shape of Food. Irregular shapes should be avoided. For instance, a leg of lamb is thick at the thigh end but thin at the shin. If cooked by microwave, the shin part will be overdone. But if the raw leg is boned, rolled, and tied, it will have a more uniform shape and will be more easily cooked.

Where unstuffed turkeys and chickens are concerned, the wings and legs should be tucked into the body shape of the bird to avoid overheating and dehydration. They may also be wrapped in light-weight aluminum foil which can be removed during the last 10 minutes of cooking time. This will allow them to be cooked to the same degree of doneness as the remainder of the bird. Be sure the foil does not touch the walls of the oven to avoid arcing.

Frozen casseroles are an easy shape and should be heated to defrost and allowed to stand for 5 minutes so that the heat may be conducted toward the center. Then the defrosted casserole should be separated with a fork and returned to the oven for the final cooking using the manufacturer's directions for heating a refrigerated casserole.

Frozen braised dishes in boilable bags may be heated like the frozen casseroles, but the bag should be shaken slightly and the top of the bag pricked to allow steam to escape. Place the bag on the serving plate and then simply tip out the contents.

Where a crisp surface is not required and the food on the plate is about even in height, the plate should be wrapped in plastic film which has been punctured to relieve the steam pressure that develops.

When making pancakes or waffles on a conventional grill—stack them, and then warm them in the microwave oven.

Timing and Quantity. The actual operation of microwave ovens is simple, but judging how long food takes to cook requires some experimentation. Each brand of oven has its own cooking guide giving approximate timing for foods. The cooking time increases with the amount of food or the number of separate items in the oven.

Additional portions call for increased heating times. Unlike the conventional oven, where six potatoes may bake at 400°F. in one hour, in the microwave oven the increased number of portions changes the cooking process. The manufacturer's instructions may vary slightly, adding half the recognized time for the first item, to doubling the original time for each item added to the oven. Experimenting with the first load will give the user the accurate time, always remembering that it is best to be underdone, therefore increasing the time by half the original time is safer than doubling it.

For each type of microwave oven there is an ideal load with

18

which the oven gives its most impressive performance. Every user should make certain that the manufacturer has clearly specified this in the manual. If two pounds is the ideal food load, then it means that the microwave oven should be capable of simultaneously heating two full-size meals on dinner plates within 1½ to 2 minutes, whereas one meal may take 1 to 1¼ minutes.

If one item takes 15 seconds to be heated in the microwave oven, then the time for bigger loads should be about as follows:

2 items	25 seconds
4 items	45 seconds
8 items	75 seconds

Conventional cooking times for raw products are often given in minutes per pound and this can sometimes also be applied to microwave cooking, using about one-fourth to one-fifth the time called for in the recipes.

Since small items cook faster than larger ones, if they are not all uniform, plan to remove the smaller items as they are done and continue to cook the larger items.

The time increase is not always proportional to the food increase since the composition of the food must be taken into consideration. If you wish to double the quantity of a recipe given in a microwave cookbook, it is best to prepare two separate dishes and bake them separately if you are not certain about the cooking time.

Browning. The brown surface color of foods is due to a chemical reaction between food sugars and amino acids. This reaction proceeds slowly at low temperatures and is accelerated by increasing the temperature. In microwave cooking, the surface temperature of foods does not change. Because of this most foods cooked in a microwave oven lack the surface coloration expected of them. These foods can be enhanced by placing them in a hot oven for a few minutes, either gas or electric, or in the case of steak and meat patties, on a grill or under a broiler.

Some manufacturers recommend the use of concentrated gravy coloring or egg white brushed on the surface.

For some foods the pale appearance does not really matter as, for instance, a cake baked in a microwave oven in 5 minutes and then covered with frosting, or a meat loaf with gravy.

Large roasts and poultry do brown in the microwave oven if the cooking time exceeds 25 minutes because the fats in the meats reach high temperatures and act to accelerate the browning reaction.

Foods in Pouches or with Skins. Frozen foods in cook-in-the-bag pouches cook well in a microwave oven, but remember to prick the top of the pouch to allow steam to escape. Foods with a skin, such as a potato, should be pierced; the same applies to egg yolk.

19

Meals
by
Microwave
Energy

This section deals with recipes prepared entirely by microwave energy.

All new cooks, and this category includes women experienced in conventional cooking who are being initiated to electronic cooking, share one goal: getting consistently good meals to the table.

Microwave energy cooking is not a mystery, as it may seem to a beginner, but preparing a meal so that everything is done and ready to serve at the same time requires a bit of adjusting to new methods and working habits.

Once the cook has mastered the basics of microwave energy cooking, she will want to branch out on her own and try even more elaborate recipes.

For perfect cooking results, recipes should be followed exactly, consulting the manufacturer's guide manual for time accuracy of the particular microwave oven in use. Here are some hints on how to succeed:

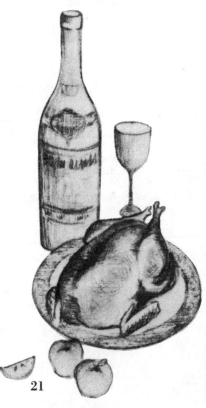

21

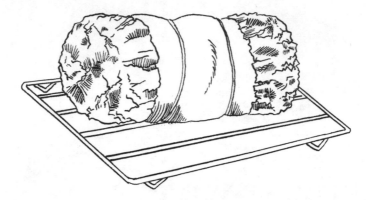

1. Read the recipe completely before you start.

2. Be sure you are familiar with the cooking terms given in the directions; if not, look them up on page 219.

3. Check the equipment you will need. If a specific size of pan is called for, and one is not available, perhaps the recipe should not be used. For instance, cake batter in too large a pan will spread too thin and the cooking time would require a change; on the other hand, batter that is poured into too small a pan will run over in baking and be undercooked.

4. Because microwave cooking is often a split-second operation, be sure you assemble all the ingredients before starting. If you have to hunt for bread crumbs or grated cheese to sprinkle over a casserole and return to the oven for a few extra seconds of heating, you have defeated your purpose of using the microwave oven as a method of quick cooking.

5. Do not alter amounts of key ingredients such as flour, eggs, liquid, and butter. You may alter salt, spices, and seasonings to your taste, if desired.

6. Do as much "ahead" preparation as possible. Chopping vegetables, fruits, or nuts takes time. But melting butter, shortening, or chocolate need not be done in advance, since your microwave oven will do it in seconds.

7. If you wish to reduce a recipe, read the amounts of ingredients carefully in order to understand how to halve them. Don't try to divide 1/3 cup by pouring out what you think is half the amount. Consult the table on page 221 and translate the amount to tablespoons and teaspoons for easier division. If the recipe calls for one egg, beat the white and yolk together with a fork until

completely blended, measure by tablespoons, and use half. Cover the remainder and store in the refrigerator and use it to supplement the breakfast scrambled eggs, the luncheon omelet, or to thicken a sauce or a pudding. Generally, depending on the size, 1 egg yields ¼ cup or 4 tablespoons.

8. When you are ready to try a recipe, you might find that you are short an ingredient. Instead of abandoning the recipe because you have no desire to run to the store just at that minute, consult the list of substitutions on page 221. You may find that you can substitute an ingredient called for in the recipe.

9. The most common problem for cooks, even when a meal is prepared in the conventional way, is how to plan the preparation of a meal so that everything is done and ready to serve at the same time. In microwave cooking the timing is even more critical since you deal with seconds and minutes instead of hours.

Until you learn to master this, try writing out your entire cooking schedule for each meal, and start cooking with the longest time required for each recipe.

10. Even cooking may require rotating the cookware. When one side of the mixture is rising or bubbling more rapidly than the other, turn the utensil.

11. If a recipe is halved or doubled, the cooking time must be adjusted.

12. Follow the recipes provided in a microwave cookbook exactly, and use the specified utensil. Later, you can try your favorite recipes by substituting the directions for a similar recipe in the book. Remember to check food for doneness at the minimum time, then follow up with another check to reach desired doneness.

13. Here is a capsule of THINGS NOT TO DO when using a microwave oven:

Do not operate the oven when it is empty because the microwave energy has no food to absorb it and the magnetron may be damaged.

Do not operate the oven when the door seal or gasket appear to be damaged. Call the manufacturer's servicing man.

Do not use metal cookware of any kind as the magnetron may be damaged.

Do not put TV dinners on aluminum trays in the oven to heat. Instead transfer the food to a serving plate.

Do not use a meat thermometer to check the food when the oven is operating. Remove the food from the oven first.

Do not wrap foods in aluminum foil to heat, except where instructions are given to use *lightweight* aluminum foil to cover spots of a turkey or roasting chicken, or other food so that they are not overcooked or dried out.

If you have children who do some cooking on conventional ranges, type out rules and instructions on how to use the microwave oven and post them near it, emphasizing to them verbally the importance of using it exactly as per instructions. If you do not think you can trust them to follow the rules, forbid them the use of the microwave oven.

14. Since you have invested money in a microwave oven, do also invest in a set of glass utility dishes to use. Here's a guide:

Suggested Glass Dishes

UTENSIL	VOLUME	APPROXIMATE SIZE	USE
Baking pans	1½ quarts 2 quarts 3 quarts	10 x 6 x 2" 12 x 8 x 2" 13 x 9 x 2"	sheet cakes, roasts, fish, to thaw frozen casseroles, poultry
Bowls	½ pint to 1 quart	graduated	to heat liquids, to scald milk or cream, sauces, puddings
Cake pans *round* *square*	about 1¾ quarts 2 quarts	8" or 9" 8" or 9"	layer cakes coffee cakes, desserts
Casseroles *with glass* *covers*	depending on recipe	1, 1½, 2, 2½ quarts	casseroles, pasta, vegetables
Cups *custard* *measuring*	depending on recipe variant	6 ounces, 10 ounces 1 cup, 2 cups	custards, cupcakes, small potpies, eggs, to heat liquids, to scald milk
Loaf pans	1½ quarts 2 quarts	8 x 4 x 3" 9 x 5 x 3"	meat loaves, loaf cakes, to cook long vegetable spears
Pie plates		8", 9", 10"	pies, meat loaves

24

Use oven-proof glass in case you may have to brown food in conventional ovens.

If you use oven-proof glass skillets, be sure they have removable handles for use in the microwave oven, as the handles are often made of metal or metal parts.

Always have glass covers available. If the utensil does not have a glass cover, use a plastic film, waxed paper, or absorbent paper.

Sauces

If you have never bothered much with sauces to dress up meats, vegetables, and even desserts, now is the time to make them a part of your cooking habits since the microwave oven has completely eliminated the difficulty, extra care, and work ordinarily required to prepare them on conventional ranges. No more constant stirring to eliminate lumps and avoid burning them.

In the tradition of French cooking, the *saucier* (sauce chef) is perhaps the most respected man in the great restaurant kitchens. Blending the broths and seasonings to make delicious aromatic sauces, he can turn even the most modestly priced cuts of meat into works of culinary art and glorify vegetables to gourmet heights. Sauces can dress up any dish and add a company touch to family meals. They garnish, extend, or bind together the foods with which they are served. And they especially contribute distinct flavors to foods cooked by microwaves.

Cooking time for sauces will vary according to the temperature of ingredients so watch them until you will be able to judge exactly when a sauce is finished.

Some sauces, especially those which contain milk, may tend to boil over rapidly, so stir them frequently, but above all be careful not to overcook them.

Basic White Sauce
(Medium)

¼ cup butter
¼ cup flour
¾ teaspoon salt
2 cups milk

1. Place butter in 1-quart glass casserole; heat in microwave oven 1 minute until melted.

2. Stir in flour and salt; blend to a smooth paste.

3. Gradually add milk, stirring constantly. Cook, uncovered, 1 minute. Stir well. Cook 2 to 3 minutes longer, stirring at the end of every 30 seconds.

Makes 2 cups.

Thin Sauce

Follow the recipe for Medium White Sauce; reduce the butter and flour to 2 tablespoons each.

Thick Sauce

Follow the recipe for Medium White Sauce; increase the butter and flour to 7-8 tablespoons each.

Béchamel Sauce

2 tablespoons butter
2 tablespoons flour
¾ teaspoon salt
⅛ teaspoon white pepper
dash thyme
2 teaspoons minced onion
1 cup chicken stock
1 cup light cream

1. Place butter in 1-quart glass casserole; heat in microwave oven 30 seconds until melted.

2. Stir in flour, salt, pepper, thyme, and onion; blend to a smooth paste.

3. Gradually add chicken stock, stirring constantly. Gradually add cream, stirring

28

constantly. Cook, uncovered, 1 minute. Stir well. Cook 2 to 3 minutes longer, stirring at the end of every 30 seconds.

Makes about 2 cups.

Beef Sauce Ramona

1. Place butter in 1-quart glass casserole; heat in microwave oven 1 minute until melted.

2. Stir in flour; blend to a smooth paste.

3. Gradually add beef broth, then milk, stirring constantly. Cook, uncovered, 1 minute.

4. Combine nonfat dry milk and water; blend to a smooth paste. Stir into sauce. Cook 2 to 3 minutes longer, stirring at the end of every 30 seconds.

5. Serve over vegetables.

Makes about 2 cups.

3 tablespoons butter
2 tablespoons flour
1 can beef broth (10½ ounces,
¼ cup milk
½ cup nonfat dry milk
¼ cup water

Belle Almondine Sauce

1. Dissolve bouillon cubes in boiling water; set aside.

2. Place butter in 1-quart glass casserole; heat in microwave oven 30 seconds until melted.

3. Add almonds; stir. Cook 30 seconds.

4. Stir in flour, salt, pepper, nutmeg, and blend to a smooth paste. Add lemon peel and blend in.

5. Gradually add bouillon, then lemon juice, and finally cream, stirring constantly until well blended. Cook, uncovered, 2 to 3 minutes, stirring at the end of every 30 seconds.

6. Serve with roast turkey, chicken, or duck.

Makes about 1½ cups.

2 chicken bouillon cubes
1 cup boiling water
1 tablespoon butter
¼ cup finely chopped almonds
2 tablespoons flour
¼ teaspoon salt
dash white pepper
dash nutmeg
¼ teaspoon grated lemon
 peel
½ teaspoon lemon juice
2 tablespoons heavy cream

29

Bordelaise Sauce

2 tablespoons butter
1 finely chopped shallot
1 clove garlic, finely minced
1 sliced onion
2 carrot slices
1 parsley sprig
6 whole peppercorns
1 whole clove
2 bay leaves
1 pinch basil
2 tablespoons flour
1 cup consommé
¼ teaspoon salt
⅛ teaspoon pepper
⅓ cup Burgundy wine
1 tablespoon finely chopped
celery tops

1. Place butter in 1-quart glass casserole; heat in microwave oven 30 seconds until melted.

2. Add shallot, garlic, onion, carrot slices, parsley, black pepper, clove, bay leaves, and basil; cook 1 minute, stirring once after 30 seconds.

3. Stir in flour until blended.

4. Gradually stir in consommé, stirring constantly until well blended. Cook, covered, 1½ to 2 minutes, stirring at the end of every 30 seconds.

5. Strain sauce; discard vegetables and spices.

6. Add salt, pepper, wine, and chopped celery tops to strained sauce; heat 30 seconds. Stir once.

7. Serve with roast beef, hamburgers, steaks, or beef casseroles.

Makes about 1¼ cups.

Broccoli-Cheese Sauce

1 package frozen chopped
broccoli (10 ounces)
1 medium onion, finely
chopped
1 tablespoon vegetable oil
1 can cream of chicken soup
(10½ ounces)
? cup processed cheese spread
½ cup light cream
1 teaspoon salt

1. Place frozen broccoli in oblong glass baking dish; heat in microwave oven 2 minutes. Turn dish around, heat 1 minute longer. Separate with fork.

2. Add onion; mix well.

3. Pour oil in 1-quart glass casserole; heat 25 seconds. Add broccoli-and-onion mixture. Cook, covered, 3 minutes, stirring at the end of each minute.

4. Add soup, stirring constantly, until blended. Cook 3 minutes, stirring at the end of each minute.

5. Add cheese, light cream, and salt; stir to blend. Cook 1½ to 2 minutes longer until sauce is bubbly.

6. Serve over hot fluffy rice or fish.

Makes about 2½ cups.

Chantilly Sauce

1. Place margarine in 1-quart glass casserole; heat in microwave oven 1 minute until melted.

2. Stir in flour and salt; blend to a smooth paste.

3. Gradually add milk, stirring constantly. Cook, uncovered, 1 minute. Stir well. Cook 2 to 3 minutes longer, stirring at the end of every 30 seconds.

4. Add nutmeg. Fold in whipped cream.

5. Serve over broccoli or asparagus spears.

Makes about 2½ cups.

¼ cup margarine
¼ cup flour
¾ teaspoon salt
2 cups milk
pinch nutmeg
½ cup heavy cream,
  whipped

Deviled Ham Sauce

1. Combine onion and butter in 1-quart glass casserole; heat in microwave oven, uncovered, 2 minutes.

2. Stir in tomato sauce, deviled ham, mustard, basil, and pepper; blend well. Cook, uncovered, 1½ minutes longer, stirring once.

3. Add parsley; stir until blended.

4. Serve over rice, omelets, or main-dish pancakes.

Makes about 2 cups.

1 medium onion,
  finely chopped
2 tablespoons butter
1 can tomato sauce
  (8 ounces)
1 can deviled ham
  (4½ ounces)
1 teaspoon dry mustard
¼ teaspoon basil
½ teaspoon pepper
2 tablespoons chopped
  parsley

31

Eastern Barbecue Sauce

2 tablespoons butter
½ clove garlic, minced
¼ cup chopped onion
½ teaspoon salt
1/8 teaspoon pepper
½ teaspoon paprika
1½ teaspoons sugar
¼ cup water
½ cup ketchup
2 tablespoons lemon juice

1. Place 1 teaspoon butter in 1-quart glass casserole.

2. Add garlic, and onion; heat in microwave oven, uncovered, 2 minutes.

3. Add salt, pepper, paprika, sugar, water, and ketchup; stir until blended. Cook, uncovered, 1½ to 2 minutes longer until sauce is bubbly.

4. Stir in lemon juice and remaining butter; mix well.

5. Serve with chicken, ham, or pork.

Makes about 1½ cups.

Eggplant Sauce Neapolitano

¼ cup olive oil
2 cloves garlic, minced
1 can Italian tomatoes
(29 ounces)
2 tablespoons chopped green olives
1 tablespoon capers
1/8 teaspoon rosemary
1 teaspoon salt
¼ teaspoon pepper
1 medium eggplant, peeled, diced

1. Pour olive oil in 1-quart glass casserole.

2. Add garlic; heat in microwave oven 1 minute.

3. Add tomatoes, olives, capers, rosemary, salt, and pepper; stir until well blended. Cook, uncovered, 3 minutes, stirring at the end of each minute.

4. Add eggplant; stir well. Cook, covered, 3 minutes, stirring at the end of each minute.

5. Serve over cooked spaghetti, spaghettini or macaroni with grated cheese.

Makes 4 servings.

Elegant Parsley Sauce

¼ cup margarine
¼ cup flour
¾ teaspoon salt
1/8 teaspoon pepper
½ cup chopped parsley
¼ cup lemon juice
2 cups milk

1. Place margarine in 1-quart glass casserole; heat in microwave oven 1 minute until melted.

2. Stir in flour, salt, pepper, and parsley; blend to a smooth paste.

3. Gradually add lemon juice, then milk, stirring constantly. Cook, uncovered, 1

32

minute. Stir well. Cook 2 to 3 minutes longer, stirring at the end of every 30 seconds.

4. Serve over asparagus, cauliflower, or carrots.

Makes about 2 cups.

English Cheese Sauce

1. Place butter in 1-quart glass casserole; heat in microwave oven 1 minute until melted.

2. Stir in flour, salt, and pepper; blend to a smooth paste.

3. Gradually add milk and cream, stirring constantly. Cook, uncovered, 1 minute.

4. Add mustard and cheese; cook 2 to 3 minutes longer, stirring at the end of every 30 seconds.

5. Serve over asparagus, broccoli, or cauliflower.

Makes about 2¼ cups.

¼ cup butter
¼ cup flour
¾ teaspoon salt
⅛ teaspoon pepper
1½ cups milk
½ cup light cream
½ teaspoon dry mustard
2 cups grated sharp Cheddar cheese

Espagnole Sauce

1. Dissolve bouillon cubes in boiling water; set aside.

2. Place butter in 1-quart glass casserole; heat in microwave oven 1 minute until melted.

3. Stir in flour; blend to a smooth paste.

4. Gradually add bouillon, stirring constantly. Add parsley, bay leaf, and thyme. Cook, uncovered, 1 minute. Cook, covered, 2 minutes longer, stirring at the end of each minute. Strain.

5. Serve with leftover roast beef, pork, or lamb.

Makes about 2¼ cups.

2 beef bouillon cubes
2 cups boiling water
3 tablespoons butter
3 tablespoons flour
2 sprigs parsley
1 small bay leaf
pinch thyme

Golden Mushroom Sauce

3 tablespoons butter
1½ tablespoons flour
1 teaspoon soy sauce
¾ cup light cream
¼ teaspoon salt
1 can chopped mushrooms,
drained (4 ounces)

1. Place butter in 1-quart glass casserole; heat 1 minute until melted.

2. Stir in flour and soy sauce; blend to a smooth paste.

3. Gradually add cream; stir until smooth. Add salt and mushrooms. Cook, uncovered, 2½ minutes, stirring at the end of every 30 seconds.

4. Serve over steaks or hamburgers.

Makes about 1½ cups.

Hollandaise Sauce

½ cup butter
4 beaten egg yolks
½ cup heavy cream
½ teaspoon salt
2 tablespoons lemon juice
1½ teaspoons prepared
mustard

1. Place butter in 1-quart glass casserole; heat in microwave oven 1 minute until melted.

2. Add egg yolks, cream, salt, and lemon juice; heat, uncovered, 1 minute, stirring at the end of every 20 seconds.

3. Stir in mustard. Remove from oven. Beat by hand until light and fluffy.

4. Serve over asparagus, broccoli, cauliflower, or Eggs Benedict.

Makes about 1¹/₃ cups.

Irish Horseradish Sauce

¼ cup margarine
¼ cup flour
¾ teaspoon salt
¹/₈ teaspoon pepper
2 cups milk
2 tablespoons prepared
horseradish
dash liquid hot-pepper
seasoning
2 teaspoons lemon juice

1. Place margarine in 1-quart glass casserole; heat in microwave oven 1 minute until melted.

2. Stir in flour, salt, and pepper; blend to a smooth paste.

3. Gradually add milk, stirring constantly. Cook, uncovered, 1 minute. Stir well.

4. Add horseradish, hot-pepper seasoning, and lemon juice; blend well. Cook 2 min-

34

utes longer, stirring at the end of every 30 seconds.

5. Serve with corned beef, boiled brisket of beef, or boiled tongue.

Makes about 2¼ cups.

Mexican Spaghetti Sauce

1. Pour oil in 2½-quart glass casserole; add onion, garlic, and celery. Heat in microwave oven 2 minutes.

2. Drain garbanzos; reserve liquid. Mash garbanzos thoroughly. Measure garbanzo liquid and add enough water to make 2½ cups. Add garbanzos and liquid to vegetable mixture. Stir until blended. Cook, uncovered, 3 minutes.

3. Add tomatoes, tomato paste, bay leaf, salt, cayenne, and oregano; stir until mixed. Cover casserole. Cook 10 minutes, stirring 3 times.

4. Serve sauce over spaghetti or macaroni.

Makes 8 servings.

3 tablespoons olive oil
1 large onion, chopped
1 clove garlic, minced
½ cup diced celery
1 can garbanzos
  (19 ounces)
water
1 can tomatoes (19 ounces)
1 can tomato paste
  (6 ounces)
1 bay leaf
1 teaspoon salt
dash cayenne
½ teaspoon oregano

Mock Hollandaise Sauce

1. Place butter in 1-quart glass casserole; heat in microwave oven 30 seconds.

2. Stir in flour and salt; blend to a smooth paste.

3. Gradually add milk, stirring constantly. Cook, uncovered, 1 minute. Stir well. Cook 1½ to 2 minutes longer, stirring at the end of every 30 seconds.

4. Beat in egg yolks, lemon juice, and margarine until well blended; heat 1 minute.

Makes about 1 cup.

2 tablespoons butter
2 tablespoons flour
½ teaspoon salt
1 cup milk
2 slightly beaten egg yolks
1 tablespoon lemon juice
2 tablespoons margarine

Mornay Sauce

¼ cup butter
¼ cup flour
¾ teaspoon salt
3 cups milk
2 slightly beaten egg yolks
2 tablespoons heavy cream
2 tablespoons grated
Parmesan cheese

1. Place butter in 1-quart glass casserole; heat in microwave oven 1 minute until melted.

2. Stir in flour and salt; blend to a smooth paste.

3. Gradually add milk, stirring constantly. Cook, uncovered, 1 minute. Stir well. Cook 1½ minutes longer, stirring at the end of every 30 seconds.

4. Add cream and cheese; stir until blended; heat 30 seconds.

5. Serve with fish.

Makes about 3 cups.

Mousseline Sauce

¼ cup butter
2 beaten egg yolks
¼ cup heavy cream
¼ teaspoon salt
1 tablespoon lemon juice
1 teaspoon prepared
mustard
¼ cup heavy cream,
whipped
dash cayenne

1. Place butter in glass bowl; heat in microwave oven 1 minute until melted.

2. Add egg yolks, cream, salt, and lemon juice; heat 1 minute, stirring 4 times.

3. Stir in mustard. Remove from oven; beat until light and fluffy.

4. Fold in whipped cream and cayenne; heat 25 seconds, stirring once. Serve over spinach, cauliflower, or broccoli.

Makes about 1 cup.

Mushroom Cheese Sauce

2 tablespoons butter
2 tablespoons flour
½ teaspoon salt
1 cup milk
½ cup shredded sharp
Cheddar cheese
1 can chopped mushrooms
with liquid (4 ounces)

1. Place butter in 1-quart glass casserole; heat in microwave oven 30 seconds.

2. Stir in flour and salt; blend to a smooth paste.

3. Gradually add milk, stirring constantly. Cook, uncovered, 1 minute. Stir well. Cook 1½ minutes longer, stirring at the end of every 30 seconds.

4. Add cheese; cook 2 or 3 minutes longer, stirring at the end of every 30 seconds.

36

5. Add mushrooms and liquid; stir until blended. Cook 1 minute longer.

6. Serve over cauliflower or green beans.

Makes about 1¾ cups.

Mustard Cream Sauce

1. Place butter in 1-quart glass casserole; heat in microwave oven 30 seconds until melted.

2. Stir in flour; blend to a smooth paste.

3. Gradually add milk, stirring constantly. Cook, uncovered, 1 minute. Stir well.

4. Add salt, pepper, mustard, and Worcestershire sauce. Cook 1½ to 2 minutes longer, stirring at the end of every 30 seconds.

5. Serve over cabbage or cauliflower.

Makes about 1 cup.

2 tablespoons butter
2 tablespoons flour
1 cup milk
½ teaspoon salt
dash pepper
1½ teaspoons prepared
  mustard
¼ teaspoon Worcestershire
  sauce

Pacific Fish Sauce

1. Place fish in shallow oblong glass dish.

2. Combine water, wine, bay leaf, onion, peppercorns, and salt; pour over fish. Cook in microwave oven 3 minutes, rotating dish once.

3. Remove fish, flake and set aside. Strain broth; reserve.

4. Place butter in 1-quart glass casserole; heat 30 seconds until melted.

5. Stir in flour; blend to a smooth paste.

6. Gradually add milk, then reserved broth, stirring constantly. Cook 3 minutes, covered.

7. Add carrot and fish; cook 1½ minutes, stirring at the end of every 30 seconds.

8. Serve over rice, red snapper, or codfish cakes.

Makes about 1¼ cups.

½ pound whitefish fillets
¼ cup water
2 tablespoons white wine
1 small bay leaf
2 tablespoons chopped onion
4 peppercorns
¾ teaspoon salt
1 tablespoon butter
1 tablespoon flour
½ cup milk
2 tablespoons grated carrot

Rajah Sauce

¼ cup butter
¼ cup chopped onion
1 cup pared, chopped apples
1 teaspoon curry powder
¼ cup flour
1¼ cups chicken broth
1 cup light cream
¾ teaspoon salt
¼ teaspoon celery salt

1. Place butter in 1-quart glass casserole; heat in microwave oven 1 minute until melted.

2. Stir in onion, apples, and curry powder; cook, covered, 3 minutes.

3. Combine flour and chicken broth; stir into onion mixture. Cook 1½ minutes, stirring at the end of every 30 seconds.

4. Add cream and salts; stir until blended. Heat 2 minutes longer, stirring once.

5. Serve over rice or chicken.

Makes about 3½ cups.

Robert Sauce

1 tablespoon butter
2 tablespoons minced onion
3 tablespoons white wine
1 tablespoon vinegar
1¼ cups Espagnole Sauce (page 33)
2 tablespoons tomato puree
1 teaspoon prepared mustard
1 tablespoon minced dill pickles
1 teaspoon chopped parsley

1. Place butter in glass bowl; heat in microwave oven 1 minute.

2. Add onion; heat 65 seconds.

3. Combine wine and vinegar; stir into butter mixture; heat 25 seconds.

4. Add Espagnole Sauce and tomato puree; heat 3 minutes.

5. Combine mustard, dill pickles, and parsley; stir into sauce. Heat 25 seconds, stirring once.

6. Serve with roast pork or pork chops.

Makes about 1¼ cups.

Sauce Belmont

3 tablespoons butter
½ cup ketchup
1 tablespoon lemon juice
1 teaspoon Worcestershire sauce
1 teaspoon prepared mustard
¼ teaspoon bottled hot-pepper sauce
2 tablespoons dry sherry wine

1. Place butter in glass bowl; heat in microwave oven 1 minute until melted.

2. Add ketchup, lemon juice, Worcestershire sauce, mustard, and hot-pepper sauce; stir until well blended. Cook 2 minutes, stirring once.

3. Add wine; heat 1 minute. Stir until smooth. Serve over Salisbury steak or corned beef.

Makes about 1 cup.

38

Shrimp Creole Sauce

1. Place butter in 1-quart glass casserole; heat 30 seconds until melted.

2. Add onion and green pepper. Cook 3 minutes, covered.

3. Stir in tomato soup, salt, pepper, and sugar; cook 1½ minutes, stirring every 30 seconds.

4. Add drained shrimp; stir to combine. Cook 2 minutes, stirring once.

5. Serve over omelet, poached fish, or croquettes.

Makes about 1½ cups.

2 tablespoons butter
¼ cup chopped onion
¼ cup chopped green pepper
1 can tomato soup
  (10½ ounces)
¼ teaspoon salt
dash pepper
1 teaspoon sugar
1 can shrimp, drained
  (5 ounces)

Soubise Sauce

1. Let onion stand in boiling water 3 minutes; drain, discard water and set onion aside.

2. Place butter in 1-quart glass casserole; heat 30 seconds until melted.

3. Stir in flour and salt; blend to make a smooth paste.

4. Gradually add milk, stirring constantly. Cook, uncovered, 1 minute. Stir well.

5. Add drained onion, nutmeg and margarine; stir to blend. Cook 2 minutes longer, stirring at the end of every 30 seconds.

6. Stir in cream; heat 1 minute.

7. Serve over potatoes, cauliflower, or fish.

Makes about 1½ cups.

1 cup finely chopped onion
1 cup boiling water
2 tablespoons butter
2 tablespoons flour
½ teaspoon salt
1½ cups milk
pinch nutmeg
1 tablespoon margarine
½ cup heavy cream

39

Texas Barbecue Sauce

2 tablespoons chopped green
pepper
2 tablespoons chopped celery
½ cup chopped onion
2 tablespoons butter
½ cup ketchup
⅓ cup wine vinegar
2 tablespoons brown sugar
¼ cup chopped sweet pickles
2½ teaspoons paprika
1 teaspoon prepared mustard

1. Place green pepper, celery, onion, and butter in 1-quart glass casserole; cook in microwave oven, uncovered, 2 minutes.

2. Combine ketchup and vinegar; stir into mixture.

3. Add brown sugar, pickles, paprika, and mustard; stir to blend. Cook 1½ minutes longer.

4. Serve sauce hot with any meat.

Makes about 1½ cups.

Dessert Sauces
Apple Merry Sauce

2 tablespoons brown sugar
1 tablespoon cornstarch
⅛ teaspoon cinnamon
⅛ teaspoon salt
1 cup apple juice
¼ cup raisins
½ cup canned apples, diced

1. Combine sugar, cornstarch, cinnamon, and salt in 1-quart glass casserole.

2. Stir in apple juice until well blended. Cook, uncovered, in microwave oven 1 minute.

3. Add raisins; cook 2 minutes, stirring every 30 seconds.

4. Add apples; stir to blend.

5. Serve hot over puddings, gingerbread, or pancakes.

Makes about 1½ cups.

Boston Hard Sauce

¾ cup sugar
3 tablespoons cornstarch
½ teaspoon salt
2 cups water
1 teaspoon vanilla
1 tablespoon butter
¼ teaspoon cinnamon
¼ teaspoon nutmeg

1. Combine sugar, cornstarch and salt in 1-quart glass casserole.

2. Stir in water; blend until smooth. Cook in microwave oven 3 minutes, stirring once after 1½ minutes.

3. Add vanilla, butter, cinnamon, and nutmeg. Blend thoroughly.

4. Serve over plum puddings and other desserts.

Makes about 2 cups.

Cantal Apricot Sauce

1. Combine preserves and orange juice in glass bowl; blend well.

2. Cook in microwave oven 1½ minutes, stirring every 30 seconds until preserves are melted.

3. Serve warm, over vanilla ice cream.

Makes about 1½ cups.

1 jar apricot preserves
(1 pound)
⅓ cup orange juice

Cardinal Sauce

1. Place frozen raspberries in a 1-quart glass casserole; heat, uncovered, in microwave oven 2 minutes.

2. Blend sugar and cornstarch; stir into raspberries.

3. Add jelly and lemon juice; cook 3 minutes, stirring well once.

4. Cool sauce before using.

5. Serve over pound cake or ice cream.

Makes about 1½ cups.

1 package frozen raspberries
(10 ounces)
½ cup sugar
2 tablespoons cornstarch
½ cup currant jelly
¼ teaspoon lemon juice

Cherry Sauce Supreme

1. Drain cherries; reserve liquid.

2. Combine sugar, cornstarch, and salt in 1-quart glass casserole.

3. Measure cherry liquid; add water, if necessary, to make ¾ cup. Stir into sugar mixture. Cook, uncovered, 2 to 2½ minutes until sauce is thick and clear, stirring 3 times.

4. Stir in butter, lemon juice, cinnamon, and cherries. Heat 45 seconds.

5. Serve warm over pound cake, pudding, or ice cream.

Makes about 1½ cups.

1 can Bing cherries
(1 pound, 2 ounces)
2 tablespoons sugar
1 tablespoon cornstarch
dash salt
water
1 tablespoon butter
½ teaspoon lemon juice
dash cinnamon

Custard Sauce Delong

4 egg yolks
¼ cup sugar
⅛ teaspoon salt
1½ cups milk
½ cup light cream
1 teaspoon rum flavoring

1. Beat egg yolks slightly with fork in a 1½-quart glass casserole.

2. Stir in sugar and salt; beat until blended.

3. Combine milk and cream; stir into egg yolk mixture. Cook in microwave oven 2½ to 3 minutes, stirring at the end of every 30 seconds. Do not overcook.

4. Add rum flavoring; stir to blend. Chill thoroughly before serving.

5. Serve over puddings.

Makes about 2¼ cups.

Dorothy's Butterscotch Sauce

1¼ cups light brown sugar
½ cup light cream
2 tablespoons light corn syrup
¼ cup butter
⅛ teaspoon salt
dash nutmeg
1 teaspoon vanilla

1. Combine sugar, cream, syrup, butter, and salt in a 1-quart glass casserole. Heat in microwave oven 2 minutes; stir and heat 2 minutes longer.

2. Add vanilla and nutmeg; stir until smooth and well blended.

3. Serve sauce warm or cold over ice cream, cake, or pudding.

Makes about 1½ cups.

Elegant Lemon Sauce

½ cup sugar
1 tablespoon cornstarch
1 cup water
2 tablespoons butter
½ teaspoon grated lemon peel
1½ tablespoons lemon juice
dash salt
¼ teaspoon lemon extract

1. Combine sugar and cornstarch in 1-quart glass casserole; stir in water. Heat, uncovered, in microwave oven, 2 minutes, stirring at the end of every 30 seconds.

2. Add butter, lemon peel, and juice; heat 20 seconds.

3. Add salt and lemon extract; stir until blended.

4. Serve warm or cold over pudding or cake.

Makes about 1¼ cups.

Grand Chocolate Sauce

1. Place chocolate in 1-quart glass casserole.

2. Pour in water; heat in microwave oven 2 to 3 minutes, turning casserole twice, back to front, until chocolate is melted.

3. Add sugar and salt; heat 30 seconds; stir until blended.

4. Add butter and vanilla and stir.

5. Serve over ice cream, cake, pudding, or canned pears.

Makes about 1⅓ cups.

3 squares unsweetened chocolate (1 ounce each)
½ cup water
¾ cup sugar
¼ teaspoon salt
4½ tablespoons butter
¾ teaspoon vanilla

Rosé Fruit Sauce

1. Place frozen raspberries in a 1-quart glass casserole. Heat, uncovered, in microwave oven 2 minutes.

2. Combine sugar and cornstarch; stir into raspberries. Heat 2 minutes, stirring well once.

3. Add wine; stir. Heat 1 minute longer.

4. Cover and chill thoroughly before using.

5. Serve over plain or pound cake.

Makes about 2 cups.

1 package frozen raspberries (10 ounces)
¼ cup sugar
2 tablespoons cornstarch
½ cup rosé wine

Quick Vanilla Sauce

3 tablespoons butter
½ cup sugar
2 slightly beaten egg yolks
½ cup boiling water
dash salt
1 teaspoon vanilla

1. Place butter in 1-quart glass casserole; heat in microwave oven 10 seconds to soften.

2. Cream butter and sugar until light and fluffy.

3. Beat in egg yolks, then boiling water, and salt. Heat, uncovered, in oven 2 minutes, stirring at the end of every 30 seconds. Do not overcook.

4. Stir in vanilla.

5. Serve hot over steamed pudding, fruit dumplings, or gingerbread.

Makes about ¾ cup.

Meats

Cooking meats successfully in the microwave oven is influenced by the following factors, just as in the conventional methods, and the guidelines to follow are quite similar in some respects:

The tenderness of a cut of meat will determine the method of cooking, i.e., roasting, stewing, braising.

The shape and size of a cut of meat will affect the cooking time.

The degree of doneness that is desired will also affect the cooking time.

In microwave roasting, there are a few more factors to be considered:

The temperature of the meat when cooking starts is important. If partially frozen, better results are obtained when the meat is heated for 5 minutes, then covered and allowed to stand for several minutes, depending on its size and the desired doneness, in order that the heat generated in the surface layers of the meat may be conducted towards the center.

45

The meat should not be salted before cooking in the microwave oven because salt absorbs the moisture of the meat and toughens the outer layer. One exception is meat cooked covered. Salt meat, as desired, after cooking. You may use other seasonings such as pepper, paprika, cayenne, herbs, and soy sauce, during cooking.

Do not place the meat on a metal roasting rack in a roaster. If you wish to raise the meat so that it does not rest in the pan drippings, place an inverted plate in the center of the pan and set the meat on top.

Cooking times in this section are based on refrigerated temperatures, about 40° F.

You may use lightweight aluminum foil to shield certain parts of the roast to prevent them from overcooking. Hold the foil in place with wooden picks and limit the areas to be covered. Do not use heavy aluminum foil. CAUTION: Be sure that the aluminum foil is not in contact with the sides of the oven or the door, otherwise arcing may result which can damage the magnetron.

A boned and rolled roast is more even in shape and will cook better.

Do not use metal skewers. Tie the meat securely with twine.

Do not serve roast immediately after it is removed from the oven. Allow it to stand, as explained on page 47. The microwave heat is still generating and the standing period is necessary as cooking continues after removal from the oven. Unlike a conventionally cooked roast which will cool when standing, the temperature of a microwave roast will rise 20° F. to 25° F. during the standing period.

Remember this at all times and do not be tempted to return the roast to the oven for a few extra minutes of cooking time because you think it is not done.

46

Always use a meat thermometer to determine doneness of the roast after removing it from the microwave oven. Check the temperature *after* the standing period is completed, beginning with the lowest time as explained on page 12.

The roasted meat should always be wrapped in aluminum foil during the standing period.

How to Roast Meat in a Microwave Oven

1. Place meat in a glass baking pan, fat side down. Recipe instructions will tell you when to turn it fat side up, if necessary.

2. Lay a sheet of waxed paper or plastic film across the top of the meat to prevent spattering inside the oven. Do not use wooden picks, or any other material, to hold it in place as these may act as paths to guide the microwaves into the meat and cause it to cook unevenly.

3. Turn baking pan around at a half-turn at the end of each ¼ of the cooking time.

4. Baste with juices while roast is cooking. The oven turns off every time you open the door, then it resumes where it left off.

5. When cooking is completed cover roast with aluminum foil, wrapping it all around, and let stand as directed in recipe.

6. Check temperature with meat thermometer while roast is standing, being careful not to touch bone or fat. If roast is to be returned to the oven for further cooking, remove aluminum foil wrapper and thermometer.

47

Roasting Chart for Beef
Based on Refrigerator Temperatures

Cut	Minutes per pound			Directions	Internal temperature taken with meat thermometer after standing time is completed		
	Rare	Medium	Well-done		Rare	Medium	Well-done
Bone-in 2-rib roast	5½	6½	7½-8	Cook for ½ of time, standing it cut side down. Turn and cook other cut side down. Let stand 30 to 40 minutes.	130-140°	150-160°	170°
3- or 4-rib roast	5½	6½	7½-8	Cover end of rib bones with foil. Cook ½ of time, fat side down. Remove foil. Turn and cook fat side up. Let stand 45 to 60 minutes.	130-140°	150-160°	170°
Boned and rolled rib, rump, sirloin tip	6½	7½	8½-9	Cover for ½ of time, fat side down. Let stand 15 to 30 minutes. If roast is twice as long as it is wide, wrap the last 2 inches of both ends with lightweight aluminum foil. Remove foil after cooking ½ of time.	130-140°	150-160°	170°

Beef

Beef Tenderloin Parisienne

1. Trim fat and connective tissue from tenderloin.

2. Place meat in glass baking pan.

3. Melt butter in microwave oven in glass container 30 seconds; spread on top of tenderloin.

4. Cook meat in microwave oven 13 to 15 minutes for medium rare.

5. Remove from oven; let stand, covered, 15 minutes, in serving platter. Uncover.

6. Sprinkle top with salt and pepper.

7. Serve with Espagnole Sauce.

Makes 4 to 6 servings.

1 beef tenderloin (3 pounds)
1 tablespoon butter
1 teaspoon salt
¼ teaspoon pepper
Espagnole Sauce (page 33)

Nikko Steak Teriyaki

1. Place steak in shallow pan.

2. Combine wine, soy sauce, Worcestershire sauce, garlic, sugar, and ginger; mix well. Pour marinade over steak. Let stand in refrigerator 24 hours, turning steak over occasionally.

3. Remove steak from sauce; place in shallow glass baking pan. Cook in microwave oven 2½ minutes on each side for medium rare; or 3 minutes each side for medium well-done.

4. Let stand 5 minutes. Sprinkle with salt and pepper.

Makes 2 servings.

1 rib steak (1¾ to 2 pounds)
¼ cup dry white wine
½ cup soy sauce
dash Worcestershire sauce
1 clove garlic, minced
2 tablespoons brown sugar
½ teaspoon ground ginger
½ teaspoon salt
¼ teaspoon pepper

Hawaiian Stew

*1 pound lean beef, cut into
2-inch cubes
½ pound veal, cut into
2-inch cubes
1 medium green pepper,
sliced
4 small ripe tomatoes,
cored
24 chunks canned pineapple,
drained
1 teaspoon salt
¼ teaspoon pepper
½ teaspoon ground ginger*

1. Divide beef, veal, green pepper, tomatoes, and pineapple equally among 4 individual glass covered casseroles.

2. Sprinkle tops with salt, pepper, and ginger.

3. Cook, covered, in microwave oven as follows:

1 serving	10 minutes
2 servings	15 minutes
3 servings	20 minutes
4 servings	25 minutes

4. Let stand 2 minutes before serving.

Makes 4 servings.

Roast Beef Juliana

*1 standing 3-rib roast of beef
(about 8-9 pounds)
¼ teaspoon marjoram
¼ teaspoon thyme
¼ teaspoon savory
½ teaspoon basil
2 beef bouillon cubes
¼ cup hot water
½ cup Burgundy wine
salt
pepper
Burgundy gravy
(page 51)*

1. Have meat at refrigerator temperature. Place in glass baking dish.

2. Combine herbs; mix well. Rub mixture into surface of meat on all sides.

3. Dissolve bouillon cubes in hot water; add wine and mix well. Baste meat.

4. Roast meat following directions on page 48, basting it frequently with wine mixture.

5. Remove meat from baking dish and let stand, wrapped in aluminum foil according to directions.

6. When ready to serve, place on serving platter. Season with salt and pepper.

7. Serve with Burgundy Gravy sauce.

Burgundy Gravy

1. After removing roasted meat from baking pan, pour drippings into bowl, leaving brown residue in baking pan.

2. Allow fat to rise to the surface; if necessary, chill in refrigerator a few minutes, Skim off fat; reserve.

3. Measure ¼ cup fat into baking pan. Stir in flour until mixture is smooth. Heat in microwave oven, uncovered, 3 minutes.

4. Add salt, pepper and enough combined wine and water to desired thickness. Cook 2 or 3 minutes, stirring at the end of each 30 seconds.

Makes about 2½ cups.

¼ cup rendered beef fat from
  drippings
3 tablespoons flour
1 teaspoon salt
¼ teaspoon pepper
Burgundy wine
water

London Broil Lord Essex

1. Trim excess fat from steak; wipe with absorbent paper. Place in glass baking pan.

2. Combine gravy concentrate, oil, lemon juice, garlic, and parsley; mix well. Spread on top of steak.

3. Cook meat in microwave oven 12 to 14 minutes for medium rare.

4. Remove from oven; let stand, covered, 15 minutes in serving platter. Uncover.

5. Sprinkle with salt and pepper. Slice meat very thinly, on diagonal across the grain.

6. Serve with Golden Mushroom Sauce.

Makes 4 to 6 servings.

1 flank steak (about 2 pounds)
1 tablespoon bottled gravy
  concentrate
1 tablespoon vegetable oil
1 teaspoon lemon juice
1 clove garlic, minced
2 teaspoons chopped parsley
1 teaspoon salt
⅛ teaspoon pepper
Golden Mushroom Sauce
  (page 34)

Corned Beef and Cabbage

*2 to 2½ pounds corned beef
brisket
1 small clove garlic
1 small onion, halved
1 whole clove
4 whole black peppers
1 small bay leaf
¼ teaspoon mustard seed
4 cups water
1 small head cabbage, cut
into wedges
4 small potatoes, pared,
quartered*

1. Place corned beef in 4-quart glass casserole.

2. Add garlic, onion, clove, peppers, bay leaf, and mustard seed.

3. Pour water over all. Cook, covered, in microwave oven 30 minutes.

4. Turn meat over; cook 10 minutes.

5. Add cabbage and potatoes; cook 5 minutes longer.

6. Let stand, covered, for 10 minutes.

7. To serve, remove corned beef, cabbage, and potatoes to serving platter. Slice corned beef and serve with horseradish or mustard.

Makes 4 servings.

Italian Steak

*1 sirloin steak (about
2 pounds),
¾ inch thick
2 tablespoons olive oil
2 tablespoons prepared garlic
spread
1 teaspoon salt
1 teaspoon rosemary
1½ teaspoons seasoned
pepper
1 cup coarse dry
bread crumbs*

1. Wipe steak with absorbent paper. Place on wooden board.

2. Combine oil, garlic spread, salt, rosemary, seasoned pepper and blend well. Spread mixture on both sides of steak.

3. Press bread crumbs into steak on both sides, using back of saucer to press deeply.

4. Place steak in shallow glass baking pan. Cover top with glass cover or plastic film; do not puncture film.

5. Cook in microwave oven 6 minutes; turn steak over. Cook 4 minutes longer.

Makes 4 servings.

Meat Loaf a la Mode

1. Pour ½ cup tomato sauce into measuring cup; set aside.

2. Combine remaining tomato sauce with beef, onion, parsley, celery, egg, bread crumbs, salt, pepper, green pepper, and mushrooms; mix well.

3. Press mixture lightly and evenly into 9-inch glass pie plate.

4. Pour reserved tomato sauce over top, spreading it evenly with a spoon. Bake, covered with punctured plastic film, 6 minutes.

5. Remove cover; bake 6 minutes longer. Let stand 10 minutes before serving.

6. To serve, cut into pie wedges and top with scoop of hot mashed potatoes.

Makes 4 to 6 servings.

1 can tomato sauce (8 ounces)
1 pound ground lean beef
2 tablespoons chopped onion
1 tablespoon minced parsley
1 tablespoon minced celery
1 slightly beaten egg
½ cup bread crumbs
½ teaspoon salt
¼ teaspoon pepper
¼ cup chopped green pepper
¼ cup chopped mushrooms
2 cups hot, seasoned, mashed potatoes

Hamburgers Galore

1. Combine beef and salt; mix well. Shape into 4 patties, ½ inch thick. Arrange patties in an 8-inch square glass baking pan so that patties do not touch each other.

2. Mix gravy coloring with water; brush top of hamburgers. Cook in microwave oven 2 minutes; turn. Brush other side with solution and cook 2 minutes longer.

3. Hamburgers will be slightly rare, but will continue to cook after they are removed from the oven. Let stand 2 minutes.

4. Spread chili sauce on one side of split hamburger buns. Place cooked hamburgers on each bun; cover with slice of cheese. Wrap each in a paper napkin or

1 pound ground lean beef
½ teaspoon salt
1 teaspoon gravy coloring
1 teaspoon water
chili sauce
cheese slices

53

absorbent paper. Place in a circle, about 1 inch apart in microwave oven. Heat 2½ minutes.

Makes 4 servings.

NOTE:
If plain hamburgers are desired, place cooked hamburgers in split bun, wrap as directed, and heat in microwave oven as directed above.

For well-done hamburgers, increase total cooking time to 5 minutes for 4.

Allow 2½ to 3½ minutes total cooking time to cook 2 hamburgers, depending on desired doneness.

To cook 1 hamburger, heat for 45 seconds.

Hong Kong Meat Loaf

2 pounds ground lean beef
1 cup soft bread crumbs
2 well-beaten eggs
½ cup finely chopped onion
½ cup finely chopped green pepper
2 tablespoons soy sauce
1 tablespoon Worcestershire sauce
2 tablespoons lemon juice
3 tablespoons brown sugar
¾ to 1 teaspoon ground ginger

1. Combine beef, bread crumbs, eggs, onion, green pepper, 1¼ tablespoons soy sauce, 2 teaspoons Worcestershire sauce, lemon juice, 2 tablespoons brown sugar and ginger; mix well.

2. Spoon into 9 x 5 x 3-inch glass loaf pan. Smooth top. Bake in microwave oven 8 minutes; turn loaf pan around and bake 7 minutes longer.

3. Combine remaining soy sauce, Worcestershire sauce and sugar; mix well. Spoon ½ of mixture over loaf and spread. Bake 8 minutes.

4. Turn loaf out onto serving platter; spoon remaining soy mixture on top. Let stand 10 minutes.

Makes about 6 servings.

Western Beef Medley

1. Combine beef and onion in 2-quart glass casserole; cook in microwave oven, covered, 3 minutes. Stir; cook 3 minutes longer.

2. Add celery, parsley, and carrots; stir.

3. Combine mushroom soup, soup can of water, bouillon cube, soy sauce, and Worcestershire sauce; pour over beef mixture. Mix well. Cook 10 minutes, stirring once.

4. Combine oregano, rice, and water; stir into meat mixture. Cover; cook 10 minutes, stirring once.

5. Let stand 10 minutes before serving.

Makes 4 to 6 servings.

1 pound ground lean beef
1 medium onion, chopped
¼ cup chopped celery
¼ cup chopped parsley
1 cup coarsely chopped carrots
1 can mushroom soup
  (10½ ounces)
1 soup can water
1 chicken bouillon cube
1 tablespoon soy sauce
1 tablespoon Worcestershire sauce
¼ teaspoon oregano
1 cup packaged, precooked rice
¾ cup water

Cheeseburger Double-Quick

1. Combine beef, onion, garlic powder, salt, and pepper; mix well.

2. Spread ½ of mixture into an 8-inch square glass baking pan.

3. Lay cheese slices over meat. Spread remaining meat mixture over cheese; smooth top.

4. Combine soy sauce with water; spread top with mixture. Cook, covered, in microwave oven 10 minutes.

5. Uncover; turn pan around back to front. Cook 6 minutes longer.

6. Let stand 5 minutes before serving.

Makes 4 servings.

1 pound ground lean beef
2 tablespoons instant minced onion
1 teaspoon garlic powder
¾ teaspoon salt
⅛ teaspoon pepper
5 slices sharp Cheddar cheese
2 tablespoons soy sauce
1 teaspoon water

Ladies' Luncheon Beef Timbales

butter
1 pound ground lean beef
½ cup light cream
1 slightly beaten egg
½ cup quick-cooking oatmeal
2 tablespoons minced green
pepper
2 tablespoons minced celery
½ teaspoon salt
dash pepper
2 teaspoons prepared
horseradish
2 teaspoons prepared mustard
6 tablespoons chili sauce

1. Butter 6 glass custard cups, about 5 ounces in volume.

2. Combine beef, cream, egg, oatmeal, green pepper, celery, salt, pepper, and horseradish; mix lightly but thoroughly. Spoon equally into custard cups. Make a hollow in center of each meat portion.

3. Combine mustard with chili sauce; mix well. Fill hollows with mixture.

4. Arrange custard cups in a circle in microwave oven. Cook 10 minutes.

5. Let stand 2 minutes. Invert cups onto serving platter. Remove cups. Let stand 3 minutes longer before serving.

Makes 6 servings.

Tijuana Chili Con Carne

2 tablespoons butter
½ cup chopped onion
¼ cup chopped green pepper
1 pound ground lean beef
1 can tomato sauce
(15 ounces)
1 can tomatoes (1 pound)
1 can kidney beans
(15 ounces), drained
1 teaspoon salt
¼ teaspoon pepper
1 tablespoon brown sugar
2 teaspoons chili powder
pinch cayenne

1. Place butter in 10-inch covered glass casserole.

2. Add onion and green pepper; cook, covered, in microwave oven 1 minute.

3. Add ground beef; cook, uncovered, 6 minutes, stirring every 2 minutes to break up meat.

4. Combine tomato sauce, tomatoes, drained kidney beans, salt, pepper, brown sugar, chili powder, and cayenne; mix well. Stir into meat mixture. Cook, covered, 5 minutes. Stir; cook 5 minutes longer.

5. Let stand 5 minutes before serving.

Makes 6 servings.

Shortcut Chow Mein

1. Separate beef into small particles in a 1-quart covered glass casserole.

2. Stir in onion; cook, covered, in microwave oven 6 minutes, stirring twice.

3. Add soup, vegetables, salt, and soy sauce; stir until well blended. Heat 5 minutes. Stir once.

4. Let stand 1 minute. Serve over chow mein noodles.

Makes 6 servings.

1 pound ground lean beef
½ cup chopped onion
1 can cream of mushroom soup
  (10½ ounces)
1 can Chinese vegetables
  (11¾ ounces)
¾ teaspoon salt
1 teaspoon soy sauce
2 cups chow mein noodles

Ravioli Meat Loaf

1. Combine beef, egg, onion, salt, bread crumbs, and milk; mix well. Divide mixture into 3 portions.

2. Place ⅓ of meat mixture in bottom of 9 x 5 x 3-inch loaf pan. Smooth top. Arrange contents of 1 can of ravioli on top. Add second layer of meat mixture; top with contents of second can of ravioli. Add remaining meat mixture; press down firmly. Bake in microwave oven 8 minutes; turn loaf pan around and bake 7 minutes longer.

3. Spread chili sauce on top. Bake 8 minutes.

4. Let stand 10 minutes before serving.

Makes 6 servings.

1½ pounds ground lean beef
1 well-beaten egg
3 tablespoons chopped onion
1 teaspoon salt
½ cup dry bread crumbs
¼ cup milk
2 cans beef ravioli
  (15½ ounces each)
2 tablespoons chili sauce

57

Tacos Mexicanos

1 tablespoon butter
1 tablespoon oil
2 cups minced onions
1 clove garlic, minced
1 pound ground lean beef
1 teaspoon salt
2 teaspoons chili sauce
¼ teaspoon powdered cumin
½ teaspoon dried oregano
1 dozen canned tortillas
½ pound shredded Cheddar
cheese
½ small head lettuce,
shredded
1 bottle taco sauce

1. Place butter in 2-quart glass casserole.

2. Add oil, onions, and garlic. Cook, covered, in microwave oven 1 minute.

3. Add ground beef; cook, uncovered, 6 minutes, stirring every 2 minutes to break up meat.

4. Add chili sauce, cumin, and oregano; mix well. Cook 1 minute longer. Keep mixture warm.

5. Place 1 tortilla at a time in shallow glass baking pan; heat in oven 30 seconds.

6. Put a spoonful of filling in each tortilla; fold in half. Add cheese and lettuce. Sprinkle with a few drops of taco sauce.

7. Wrap tortillas in paper napkins; heat each tortilla 20 seconds.

Makes 12 tortillas.

Hungarian Stew

1 pound ground lean beef
3 cups medium-size egg
noodles, uncooked
1 cup bouillon
1 cup water
1 can tomato sauce
(8 ounces)
1 envelope onion soup mix
(1½ ounces)
½ teaspoon salt
¾ teaspoon paprika

1. Place ground beef in 2½-quart glass casserole. Cook, covered, in microwave oven 7 minutes, stirring twice to separate the meat. Drain off excess fat.

2. Add noodles over meat.

3. Combine bouillon, water, tomato sauce, and soup mix; mix well. Pour over noodles. Cook, covered, 10 minutes. Turn casserole around; cook 5 minutes longer, stirring twice.

4. Add salt and paprika; stir once. Let stand 5 minutes.

Makes 4 servings.

58

Corned-Beef Hash Americana

1. Remove corned-beef hash from cans; spoon into 4 individual glass casseroles. Make a well in the center of each portion with back of spoon.

2. Break 1 egg into each center. Cover with waxed paper resting lightly on top. Cook in microwave oven 6 to 6½ minutes or until eggs are set to desired doneness.

3. Sprinkle with salt and pepper.

4. Combine water and ketchup; spoon a little of the mixture over each egg.

Makes 4 servings.

2 cans corned-beef hash
(1 pound each)
4 eggs
1 teaspoon salt
¼ teaspoon pepper
1 tablespoon water
2 tablespoons ketchup

English Creamed Beef

1. Place butter in 1-quart glass casserole; heat in microwave oven 1 minute until melted.

2. Stir in flour; blend to a smooth paste. Cook 1 minute.

3. Gradually stir in milk, then cream, stirring constantly until smooth. Cook 4 minutes, stirring three times.

4. Tear beef into pieces; add to sauce. Season with pepper. Heat 1 minute.

5. Serve over toast.

Makes 4 servings.

3 tablespoons butter
3 tablespoons flour
1 cup milk
½ cup light cream
1 jar dried beef (4 ounces)
¼ teaspoon pepper
4 slices toasted white bread

Chipped Beef in Sour Cream

1 jar dried beef (4 ounces)
1 tablespoon butter
1 pint sour cream
¼ cup dry white wine
1 tablespoon grated Parmesan
cheese
dash cayenne
1 can artichoke hearts
(8½ ounces),
drained, halved

1. Rinse dried beef under running cold water. Dry thoroughly on absorbent paper. Tear into pieces.

2. Place butter in 1-quart glass casserole; heat in microwave oven 1 minute until melted.

3. Add sour cream, wine, cheese, and cayenne; mix well.

4. Gently stir in artichoke hearts and dried beef. Heat, covered, 2 minutes, stirring occasionally.

5. Let stand 2 minutes.

Makes 4 servings.

Hot Dog in a Bun

4 frankfurters
4 frankfurter rolls
mustard

1. Place 1 frankfurter in each roll.

2. Spread with mustard, if desired.

3. Wrap in paper napkin or paper towel. Heat each frankfurter 30 seconds. Or, arrange 4 in a circle, about an inch apart. Heat 1½ minutes.

Veal

Roasting Chart for Veal

For Rolled Roast: Based on Refrigerator Temperature

Minutes per pound	Directions	Internal temperature taken with meat thermometer after standing time is completed
9½-10	Place 3 slices of bacon across top of roast. Cook ½ of time. Turn and cook on other side, placing 3 fresh bacon slices across top. Let stand 30 minutes.	165°-170°

Roast Leg of Veal

1 boneless leg of veal, rolled
(4 to 5 pounds)
2 cloves garlic, split
2 tablespoons soy sauce
6 slices bacon
1 teaspoon salt
¼ teaspoon pepper

1. Have meat at refrigerator temperature. Place in glass baking pan.

2. Rub meat well with cut garlic; discard garlic.

3. Brush with soy sauce. Arrange 3 slices of bacon to cover top. Roast meat following directions on page 61, using remaining 3 slices of bacon on other side.

4. Remove meat from baking dish and let stand, wrapped in aluminum foil.

5. When ready to serve, season with salt and pepper.

Makes 8 servings.

Veal Loaf Italiano

2 eggs
¾ cup milk
½ cup ketchup
1 cup packaged cracker meal
½ cup chopped stuffed olives
1½ teaspoons salt
¼ teaspoon pepper
pinch thyme
1 tablespoon butter
¼ cup chopped onion
1½ pounds ground veal
½ pound lean ground pork
1 tablespoon Worcestershire
sauce
Sauce Belmont (page 38)

1. Beat eggs slightly; stir in milk, ketchup, cracker meal, olives, salt, pepper, and thyme; set aside.

2. Place butter in glass bowl; heat in microwave oven 30 seconds until melted.

3. Add onion. Cook, covered, 2 minutes. Add to egg mixture along with veal and pork. Mix until well combined.

4. Pack mixture lightly and evenly in 9-inch square glass pan; brush top with Worcestershire sauce. Bake 12 minutes.

5. Let stand 10 minutes before serving.

6. To serve, cut into 6 squares, remove from pan onto serving platter, and serve with Sauce Belmont.

Makes 6 servings.

Veal Loaf

1. Combine veal, pork butt, bread crumbs, cream, eggs, and salt.

2. Place onion, celery, parsley, green pepper, and butter in glass bowl. Cook, covered, 2 minutes, stirring once. Add to meat mixture. Mix until well combined.

3. Pack mixture into 9 x 5 x 3-inch glass loaf pan; brush top with soy sauce. Bake 14 minutes.

4. Let stand 10 minutes before serving.

5. Serve sliced with Bordelaise Sauce.

Makes 4 to 6 servings.

1 pound ground veal
1 pound ground pork butt
1 cup bread crumbs
½ cup cream, light or heavy
3 well-beaten eggs
1½ teaspoons salt
1 medium onion, chopped
2 stalks celery, chopped
1 teaspoon chopped parsley
½ green pepper, chopped
1 tablespoon butter
1 tablespoon soy sauce
Bordelaise Sauce (page 30)

Veal a la King

1. Place butter in 2½-quart glass casserole; heat in microwave oven 1 minute until melted.

2. Add green pepper. Cook, covered, 2 minutes.

3. Stir in flour; blend to a smooth paste.

4. Add salt and pepper. Gradually add chicken broth, then soup, stirring constantly until well blended and smooth.

5. Add veal; cook, covered, 7 minutes.

6. Combine egg yolks and milk; stir into hot veal mixture. Cook 1 minute, stirring once.

7. Add pimiento and wine; stir to blend.

8. Let stand 5 minutes. Serve over rice, toast, or buttered noodles.

Makes 6 servings.

¼ cup butter
¼ cup thinly sliced green
  pepper
¼ cup flour
¾ teaspoon salt
⅛ teaspoon pepper
1 cup chicken broth
1 can mushroom soup
  (10½ ounces)
2 cups cubed cooked veal
2 slightly beaten egg yolks
½ cup milk
2 tablespoons slivered pimiento
2 tablespoons sherry wine

Veal Marengo

1 can tomatoes
(1 pound, 3 ounces)
1 package dried spaghetti-
sauce mix (1½ ounces)
½ cup canned chicken gravy
1 teaspoon instant minced
onion
½ teaspoon salt
dash pepper
2 tablespoons vegetable oil
2 cups cubed cooked veal
½ teaspoon rosemary

1. In 2-quart glass casserole combine tomatoes, spaghetti sauce mix, chicken gravy, onion, salt, pepper, and oil; stir until well blended. Cook, covered, in microwave oven 10 minutes, stirring 3 times.

2. Add veal and rosemary; cook 3 minutes longer. Stir.

3. Serve over toast or hot rice.

Makes 4 to 6 servings.

Lamb
Roasting Chart for Lamb
Based on Refrigerator Temperature

Cut	Minutes per pound: Medium	Well-done	Directions	Internal temperature taken with meat thermometer after standing time is completed Medium	Well-done
Leg	7-7½	8-8½	If shank bone of	160°-170°	175°-180°
Shoulder			leg has not been removed, wrap last 2 inches with foil. Cook roast ¼ time, fat side down, ¼ time fat side up. Remove foil. Repeat cooking, placing roast fat side up and down. Let stand 30 to 45 minutes.		

Greek Minted Lamb

1. Combine orange juice concentrate, lime juice, butter, oil, and salt in 1½-quart glass casserole. Heat, uncovered, in microwave oven 3 minutes, stirring once.

2. Place lamb in shallow glass baking pan; brush with orange mixture. Roast lamb 35 minutes, turning around and brushing with orange sauce, every 5 minutes.

3. Remove from oven; let meat stand wrapped in aluminum foil for 30 minutes.

4. Add celery, parsley, hazelnuts, and mint flakes to remaining orange sauce. Cook, uncovered, 5 minutes, stirring once.

5. To serve: slice meat on serving platter. Spoon some of the sauce over it, serve remainder on the side.

Makes 4 to 6 servings.

1 can frozen orange juice concentrate (6 ounces)
¼ cup lime juice
2 tablespoons butter
2 tablespoons olive oil
½ teaspoon salt
1 shoulder of lamb (about 4 pounds)
2 tablespoons chopped celery
2 tablespoons chopped parsley
½ cup chopped hazelnuts
1 tablespoon dry mint flakes

Roast Leg of Lamb

1 leg of lamb (about 5 pounds)
1 clove garlic, slivered
½ cup vegetable oil
2 cups dry red wine
3 medium onions, sliced
¼ teaspoon cloves
2 teaspoons salt
1 teaspoon oregano
½ teaspoon thyme
½ teaspoon basil
1 tablespoon chopped parsley

1. Wipe lamb with damp absorbent paper. Make several small pockets in flesh with small knife; insert garlic slivers. Place meat in shallow glass baking dish.

2. Combine remaining ingredients; mix well. Pour marinade over meat.

3. Cover; refrigerate 48 hours, turning lamb occasionally.

4. Remove lamb from marinade. Place in glass baking dish. Wrap last 2 inches of shank bone of leg with aluminum foil.

5. Roast, uncovered, according to directions on page 65, basting meat occasionally with marinade.

6. When done, let stand as directed.

Makes 8 servings.

Lamb Loaf Bombay

1 egg
1 cup milk
1 cup dry bread crumbs
1 tablespoon chopped parsley
1 cup grated raw carrot
1 tablespoon chopped celery
1 tablespoon lemon juice
2 teaspoons salt
½ teaspoon garlic powder
½ teaspoon poultry seasoning
¼ teaspoon pepper
2½ pounds ground lean lamb
1½ teaspoons soy sauce
Rajah Sauce (page 38)

1. Beat egg slightly with fork; stir in milk.

2. Add bread crumbs, parsley, carrot, celery, lemon juice, salt, garlic powder, and poultry seasoning; blend well.

3. Combine with pepper and lamb; mix thoroughly.

4. Pack mixture into a 9 x 5 x 3-inch glass loaf dish. Smooth top. Brush with soy sauce. Bake in microwave oven 14 minutes.

5. Let stand 10 minutes before serving.

6. Serve with Rajah Sauce.

Makes about 6 servings.

Southern Lamb Spareribs

1. Place spareribs in single layer in shallow glass baking pan.

2. Combine soy sauce, chili sauce, molasses, wine, onion, garlic, and thyme. Pour over meat.

3. Cover; refrigerate 3 hours.

4. Remove meat to glass baking pan. Drain marinade; reserve.

5. Roast lamb ribs in microwave oven, uncovered, 3 minutes. Turn ribs over; cook 3 minutes longer. Brush with marinade. Cook 2 minutes. Turn ribs once again, brush with marinade, cook 2 minutes longer.

6. Let stand 10 minutes.

Makes 2 servings

1 pound lamb spareribs
¼ cup soy sauce
¼ cup chili sauce
1 tablespoon molasses
1 tablespoon sherry wine
1½ tablespoons chopped onion
1 small clove garlic, minced
pinch thyme

Hurry Lamb Curry

1. Place butter in 1½-quart glass casserole.

2. Add onion, celery, and green pepper. Cook, covered, in microwave oven 2 minutes.

3. Stir in chicken gravy.

4. Add lamb, curry powder, apple, and salt. Cook, covered, 10 minutes, rotating casserole once.

5. Let stand 5 minutes.

Makes 4 servings.

2 tablespoons butter
¼ cup coarsely chopped onion
¼ cup thinly sliced celery
¼ cup chopped green pepper
1 cup canned chicken gravy
1½ cups cubed cooked lamb
¾ teaspoon curry powder
½ cup pared, diced apple
¼ teaspoon salt

Poorman's Lamb Stew

1. Combine carrots, onions, potatoes, salt, and water in 2-quart glass casserole. Cook, covered, in microwave oven 5 minutes.

2. Add gravy, lamb, pepper, and thyme; stir to blend well. Cook, covered, 10 minutes, stirring once and rotating casserole once.

3. Let stand 5 minutes before serving.

Makes 4 servings.

1 cup sliced carrots
1 cup sliced onions
1 cup cubed potatoes
¾ teaspoon salt
½ cup water
1 cup leftover lamb gravy
2 cups cubed cooked lamb
⅛ teaspoon pepper
pinch thyme

Lamb-Stuffed Peppers

4 medium green peppers
1 cup diced, cooked lamb
1 cup cooked rice
1 can tomato sauce (8 ounces)
½ teaspoon oregano
1 teaspoon garlic salt
1 tablespoon minced onion
¼ cup finely chopped celery

1. Wash peppers, remove seeds and membrane. Parboil in salted, boiling water 4 minutes; drain.

2. Combine lamb, rice, tomato sauce, oregano, garlic salt, onion, and celery; mix thoroughly.

3. Stuff peppers with mixture. Place in 1½-quart glass casserole. Bake in microwave oven 10 minutes.

4. Let stand 3 minutes.

Makes 4 servings.

Citrus-Glazed Lamb Roast

1 boned shoulder of lamb
(5 pounds), rolled, tied
2 tablespoons flour
1 teaspoon salt
¼ teaspoon pepper
¾ cup orange marmalade
¼ cup lemon juice
1 tablespoon parsley,
chopped

1. Place meat in glass baking pan. Roast in microwave oven, according to directions on page 65.

2. Combine, flour, salt, pepper, marmalade, lemon juice, and 1 teaspoon parsley; blend to a smooth paste.

3. After lamb has been turned fat side up, spread marmalade mixture on meat. Continue cooking as directed. Sprinkle with parsley.

4. When done, let stand, wrapped in aluminum foil, to desired doneness.

Makes 6 to 8 servings.

English Lamb Chops

1. Combine lemon peel, oregano, basil, garlic powder, and pepper; mix well. Rub mixture over entire surface of meat.

2. Place butter in 2-quart glass oblong baking pan; heat in microwave oven 30 seconds until melted. Stir in onion; cook 2 minutes.

3. Place lamb chops in single layer in baking pan, spooning some of the onions on top of them. Cook, uncovered, 15 minutes, turning over each chop after the first 10 minutes, and rotating dish once.

4. Arrange carrots around the meat; pour vermouth over meat. Cover pan with plastic film, punctured in center. Cook 7 minutes longer until carrots are tender. Season with salt.

5. Pour off some of the pan drippings into a measuring cup; stir in cornstarch and return to pan. Cook 2 minutes. Sprinkle with shallot.

Makes 4 servings.

2 teaspoons grated lemon peel
½ teaspoon oregano
½ teaspoon basil
¼ teaspoon garlic powder
⅛ teaspoon pepper
4 lamb shoulder chops. 1¼ inches thick
1 tablespoon butter
1 large onion, thinly sliced
4 carrots, pared, sliced
2 tablespoons dry vermouth
½ teaspoon salt
1 teaspoon cornstarch
1 tablespoon chopped shallot

Scottish Lamb Stew

1. Arrange alternate layers of potatoes, lamb, and onions in 3-quart glass casserole.

2. Sprinkle with salt, pepper, and thyme.

3. Add bay leaves.

4. Pour water over all. Cook, covered, in microwave oven, 20 minutes, stirring twice during cooking, and rotating casserole once.

5. Let stand 5 minutes before serving.

Makes 6 to 8 servings.

4 pounds potatoes, pared, cut into quarters
2 pounds lamb neck slices
1 pound onions, thickly sliced
1 teaspoon salt
¼ teaspoon pepper
½ teaspoon thyme
2 bay leaves
2 cups water

Florida Lamb Steaks

2 lamb steaks (about 2
pounds), cut in halves
1 teaspoon salt
2 medium oranges, sliced
2 tablespoons brown sugar
1 tablespoon grated orange
peel
½ teaspoon ginger
¼ teaspoon cloves
1 teaspoon dried mint
flakes
pinch thyme
¼ cup melted butter

1. Arrange meat in shallow glass baking pan in single layer.

2. Sprinkle with salt. Top with oranges.

3. Combine brown sugar, orange peel, ginger, cloves, mint flakes, thyme, and butter; mix thoroughly. Pour over lamb and oranges. Bake, covered, in microwave oven 10 minutes.

4. Turn each lamb steak over once, and rotate baking pan. Bake, covered, 10 to 12 minutes longer, basting 3 or 4 times.

5. Let stand 15 minutes before serving.

Makes 4 servings.

Swedish Boiled Lamb

1 shoulder of lamb
(2½ to 3 pounds)
boiling water
2 teaspoons salt
4 peppercorns
1 bay leaf
5 dill sprigs
Espagnole Sauce
(page 33)

1. Scald meat in boiling water. Drain. Place in 2-quart oblong glass baking dish. Add boiling water to barely cover meat.

2. Add salt, peppers, bay leaf, and dill. Cover top of pan with plastic film; puncture center to allow steam to escape. Cook in microwave oven 20 minutes, turning meat over after the first 9 minutes, and rotating pan once.

3. Remove meat to serving platter; cover and let stand 10 minutes.

4. Serve with Espagnole Sauce.

Makes 4 servings.

Indonesian Lamb Curry

1. Place butter in 2-quart glass casserole; heat in microwave oven 30 seconds until melted.

2. Add lima beans, lamb gravy, onion, mace, salt, and pepper; mix well. Cook, covered, 4 minutes.

3. Add lamb, shredded lettuce, and curry powder; stir gently to mix well. Cook, covered, 3 minutes.

4. Remove from oven; let stand 10 minutes before serving.

5. Serve over hot rice.

Makes 4 servings.

2 tablespoons butter
1 cup cooked lima beans
2 cups leftover lamb gravy
1 teaspoon instant onion
¼ teaspoon mace
¾ teaspoon salt
¼ teaspoon pepper
2 cups diced cooked lamb
1 small head lettuce, shredded
1 teaspoon curry powder
2 cups hot cooked rice

Polish Stew

1. Arrange bacon in 2-quart glass casserole; heat in microwave oven 3 minutes.

2. Add onion; cook 2 minutes, stirring once.

3. Add sauerkraut, salt, pepper, and caraway seed; cook 3 minutes.

4. Add lamb; cook, covered, 5 minutes.

5. Add sausage; cook, uncovered, 1 minute.

6. Let stand 10 minutes before serving.

Makes 4 servings.

4 strips bacon, diced
1 medium onion, minced
3 cups sauerkraut
½ teaspoon salt
¼ teaspoon pepper
1 tablespoon caraway seed
2½ cups diced cooked lamb
¼ pound sliced Polish sausage

Indian Lamb Curry

3 tablespoons butter
2 medium onions, sliced
¾ teaspoon ground ginger
2 pounds boneless lean lamb,
    cut into ¾-inch cubes
4 teaspoons powdered
    turmeric
1 cup yogurt
2 tablespoons water
¾ cup heavy cream
1 cup ground almonds
¾ teaspoon salt
¼ teaspoon chili powder
2 bay leaves

1. Place 1½ tablespoons butter in 2-quart glass casserole; heat in microwave oven 1 minute until melted.

2. Add onions and ginger; cook 2 minutes.

3. Add lamb, 2 teaspoons turmeric, and ½ cup yogurt. Cook, uncovered, 1 minute, stirring once.

4. Add remaining yogurt and water; cook, covered, 7 minutes.

5. Combine cream, almonds, salt, chili powder, and remaining turmeric. Add to meat mixture along with bay leaves. Cook, covered, 3 minutes, stirring once.

6. Let stand 10 minutes before serving.

Makes 4 servings.

Gourmet Lamb Loaf

3 cups ground cooked lamb
2 well-beaten eggs
1 can tomato sauce
    (8 ounces)
⅓ cup chopped cashew nuts
⅓ cup diced currants
½ teaspoon salt
⅛ teaspoon cloves
⅛ teaspoon cinnamon
⅛ teaspoon allspice
Rajah Sauce (page 38)

1. Combine lamb, eggs, tomato sauce, cashew nuts, currants, salt, cloves, cinnamon, and allspice; mix thoroughly.

2. Pack mixture into an 8 x 4 x 3-inch glass loaf pan. Smooth top. Cover with plastic film, punctured in center to allow steam to escape. Bake in microwave oven 14 minutes.

3. Let stand 10 minutes before serving.

4. Serve with Rajah Sauce.

Makes 4 servings.

Lamburgers Tarragon

1. Drain peaches; set aside and reserve syrup.

2. Combine lamb, egg, bread crumbs, seasoned salt, pepper, tarragon, soy sauce, parsley, garlic, milk, and 2 tablespoons peach syrup; mix thoroughly with fork.

3. Shape into 6 patties; place in shallow glass baking pan in single layer, about ¾-inch apart. Cover with plastic film, punctured in center to allow steam to escape. Bake in microwave oven 8 minutes. Turn each patty over; bake 7 minutes longer.

4. Combine remaining peach syrup, cinnamon, and cloves; pour over lamburgers. Top each with a peach half. Bake, uncovered, 2 minutes.

5. Let stand 5 minutes before serving.

Makes 6 servings.

1 can peach halves
  (1 pound)
1½ pounds ground lamb
1 slightly beaten egg
½ cup fine, dry bread crumbs
1 teaspoon seasoned salt
¼ teaspoon pepper
¼ teaspoon dried tarragon
½ teaspoon soy sauce
2 tablespoons chopped
  parsley
3 cloves garlic, minced
¼ cup milk
¼ teaspoon cinnamon
⅛ teaspoon powdered cloves

Pork and Ham
Roasting Chart for Pork and Ham
Based on Refrigerator Temperature

Cut	Minutes per pound	Directions	Internal temperature taken with meat thermometer after standing time is completed
Pork, fresh loin	8-8½	Cook for ½ of time fat side down. Turn and cook fat side up. Let stand 15 to 20 minutes. If roast is more than twice as long as wide, wrap last 2 inches of both ends with foil. Remove foil after cooking ½ of time.	170°
Ham, shoulder	9½-10	Cook for ½ of time fat side down. Turn and cook fat side up. Let stand 30 to 45 minutes.	185°

73

Canned hams 3 to 5 pounds	6	Remove gelatin from ham. Cook ½ of time fat side down. Turn and cook fat side up. Glaze, if desired, during last 5 minutes. Let stand 20 to 30 minutes.	130°
8 to 10 pounds	5	Remove gelatin from ham. Cook ½ of time fat side down. Turn and cook fat side up. Glaze, if desired, during last 5 minutes. Let stand 40 to 45 minutes.	130°
Ready or fully cooked ham (half)	7	Start cooking fat side down. Divide total cooking time by 4. Turn ham 4 times. Glaze, if desired, during last 5 minutes. Let stand 30 to 60 minutes.	130°

Polish Pork and Sauerkraut

1 boneless pork shoulder roast (2 pounds), trimmed
2 cups chopped onions
1 clove garlic, minced
1 teaspoon dried dill
1 teaspoon caraway seeds
1 tablespoon butter
1 beef bouillon cube
½ cup hot water
2½ teaspoons salt
1 can sauerkraut (1 pound, 11 ounces), drained
2 cups dairy sour cream
1 tablespoon paprika

1. Cut pork into 2-inch cubes; set aside.

2. Combine onions, garlic, dill, caraway seed, and butter in a 2½-quart glass casserole; heat in microwave oven 2 minutes, stirring once.

3. Dissolve bouillon cube in hot water; add to onion mixture. Add pork cubes, and salt. Mix well. Cook, covered, 10 minutes, stirring twice, rotating casserole once.

4. Add drained sauerkraut; mix well. Cook, covered, 3 minutes.

5. Stir in sour cream and paprika. Cook 1 minute.

6. Let stand 10 minutes before serving.

Makes 6 servings.

74

Polynesian Spareribs

1. Wipe spareribs with damp absorbent paper.

2. Combine flour, salt, pepper, and paprika; mix well. Dredge spareribs in mixture. Arrange spareribs in large shallow glass baking pan.

3. Combine crushed pineapple, orange marmalade, soy and Worcestershire sauces, and sugar; blend well.

4. Combine lemon juice and wine; beat lightly with fork to blend.

5. Add ginger, and onion and garlic powders; add to pineapple mixture, blending well.

6. Spoon 5 tablespoons of sauce over ribs; bake, uncovered, in microwave oven 32 minutes, turning ribs 4 times during cooking.

7. Drain off pan liquid; discard.

8. Pour remaining pineapple sauce over ribs; cook 10 to 14 minutes longer until ribs are tender and browned, turning and basting twice.

9. Let stand 15 minutes before serving.

Makes 4 to 6 servings.

4 pounds pork spareribs, cut into serving pieces
¼ cup flour
1 teaspoon salt
¼ teaspoon pepper
¼ teaspoon paprika
1 can crushed pineapple (8½ ounces)
¼ cup orange marmalade
3 tablespoons soy sauce
1 teaspoon Worcestershire sauce
1 tablespoon brown sugar
1 tablespoon lemon juice
1 tablespoon sherry wine
½ teaspoon powdered ginger
¼ teaspoon onion powder
¼ teaspoon garlic powder

Southern Pork Hocks

1. Place pork hocks in 2½-quart glass casserole.

2. Pour water over meat. Add lima beans, salt, pepper, caraway seed, and mace. Cook, covered, in microwave oven 30 minutes.

3. Turn hocks over; stir beans, rotate casserole; cook 15 minutes longer.

4. Let stand, covered, 10 minutes before serving.

Makes 2 servings.

2 pork hocks, cracked
4 cups water
1 cup dried lima beans
2 teaspoons salt
¼ teaspoon pepper
½ teaspoon caraway seed
pinch mace

75

Texas Barbecued Spareribs

1 pound pork spareribs, cut
into serving pieces
½ cup Texas Barbecue Sauce
(page 40)
1 teaspoon chili powder
2 tablespoons lemon juice

1. Place spareribs in large shallow glass baking pan. Bake, uncovered, in microwave oven 4 minutes.

2. Turn spareribs over. Pour ¼ cup Texas Barbecue Sauce on top. Bake 2 minutes.

3. Turn spareribs over again. Sprinkle with chili powder and lemon juice. Pour remaining sauce on top. Bake 4 to 6 minutes, testing spareribs for doneness, until fork tender.

Makes 2 servings.

Chili-Dilly Casserole

1 pound ground lean pork
1 teaspoon margarine
1 can chili con carne
(15 ounces)
2 tablespoons minced green
pepper
1 teaspoon minced parsley
2 cups crisp corn chips
1 medium onion, chopped
1 cup grated sharp
Cheddar cheese

1. Place pork and margarine in 2-quart glass casserole; cook, uncovered, in microwave oven 3 minutes, stirring twice. Drain excess fat.

2. Add chili con carne, green pepper, and parsley; stir well. Cook, covered, 3 minutes.

3. Place 1 cup of corn chips in a 9-inch glass baking pan.

4. Arrange ½ chopped onion and ½ of the cheese over corn chips. Pour hot chili over top; arrange remaining onions on chili, then remaining corn chips. Sprinkle with cheese.

5. Cover pan with plastic film, punctured in center to allow steam to escape. Cook 4½ minutes until chili is bubbly.

6. Let stand 5 minutes before serving.

Makes 4 servings.

German Pork Hocks

1. Place pork hocks in 2½-quart glass casserole.

2. Pour water over meat. Add salt, bay leaf, and ¼ cup sauerkraut. Cook, covered, in microwave oven 30 minutes.

3. Turn hocks over; add remaining sauerkraut, caraway seed, and apple; stir well. Cook 15 minutes longer. Strain off some of the liquid.

4. Let stand, covered, 10 minutes before serving.

Makes 2 servings.

2 pork hocks (about 1½ to 2 pounds)
4 cups water
½ teaspoon salt
1 bay leaf
1½ cups canned sauerkraut, undrained
½ teaspoon caraway seed
1 small tart apple, pared, cored, cut into wedges

Pennsylvania Dutch Roast Pork

1. Place pork, fat side down, in shallow glass baking pan. Bake in microwave oven according to directions on page 74.

2. When meat is done remove to serving platter; wrap in aluminum foil and let stand according to directions.

3. Pour off all but 1 tablespoon of fat from pan, leaving meat drippings. Add onion; cook 2 minutes.

4. Add flour, salt, pepper, sage, thyme, basil, and gravy coloring; blend to a smooth paste.

5. Gradually add water, stirring constantly until thickened. Return to microwave oven; heat gravy 3 to 4 minutes, stirring occasionally until bubbly.

Makes 6 to 8 servings.

1 loin of pork (about 3½ pounds)
1 tablespoon minced onion
2 tablespoons flour
1 teaspoon salt
⅛ teaspoon pepper
1 teaspoon sage
¼ teaspoon thyme
¼ teaspoon basil
¼ teaspoon gravy coloring
1½ cups water

77

Pork Loaf Par Excellence

1¾ cups soft bread crumbs
½ cup milk
1 slightly beaten egg
2 tablespoons minced onion
1 tablespoon chopped parsley
1 tablespoon chopped celery
2 pounds ground lean pork
1½ teaspoons salt
⅛ teaspoon pepper
½ teaspoon rosemary
¼ teaspoon thyme
1 can tomato sauce (8 ounces)
¼ teaspoon oregano

1. Combine bread crumbs and milk in bowl; let stand 5 minutes.

2. Add egg, onion, parsley, and celery; stir to blend.

3. Add meat, salt, pepper, rosemary, and thyme; mix thoroughly.

4. Pack mixture lightly into a 9 x 5 x 3-inch glass loaf pan.

5. Combine tomato sauce and oregano; beat with fork to blend. Pour ½ cup tomato sauce evenly over top. Bake in microwave oven 14 minutes.

6. Let stand 10 minutes before serving. Pour off excess fat.

7. Heat remaining tomato sauce in microwave oven 2 or 3 minutes until bubbly. Serve with meat loaf.

Makes about 6 to 8 servings.

Louisiana Pork Chops

6 rib pork chops (about 1½ pounds)
2 large onions, sliced
1 can tomato soup (10½ ounces)
½ teaspoon Tabasco sauce
½ teaspoon salt
¼ teaspoon marjoram

1. Trim pork chops of excess fat. Place in shallow glass baking pan in 1 layer.

2. Top with onions.

3. Combine tomato soup, Tabasco, salt, and marjoram; blend thoroughly. Pour over chops and onions. Bake, covered, in microwave oven 10 minutes.

4. Turn chops over, spooning onions and sauce on top. Bake 10 minutes longer until fork tender.

5. Let stand 5 minutes before serving.

Makes 4 to 6 servings.

Pork Choucroute

1. Place in 1 layer in bottom of a shallow glass baking pan; heat in microwave oven 3 minutes. Drain excess fat.

2. Place sauerkraut on top of bacon in 1 layer.

3. Add pork chops on top.

4. Combine onion, peppercorns, berries, bouillon, and wine; blend thoroughly. Pour over pork chops. Cover baking pan with plastic film, punctured in center to allow steam to escape. Bake, covered, 10 minutes.

5. Turn chops over, spooning sauce on top. Bake 10 to 12 minutes longer.

6. Let stand 10 minutes before serving.

Makes 6 servings.

6 slices bacon
1 can sauerkraut (1 pound, 11 ounces), drained
6 pork chops, rib or loin
1 medium onion, sliced
12 peppercorns
2 juniper berries
2 cups bouillon
1 cup dry white wine

Southern Glazed Ham

1. Place ham, fat side down, in shallow glass baking pan. Bake in microwave oven according to directions on page 74.

2. 20 minutes before cooking is completed, remove ham from oven. With tip of knife, cut off and remove rind. Cut into fat making a diamond pattern and being careful not to cut into ham. Insert cloves, placing only 5 cloves on top of thickest part of ham. Return to oven and bake specified remaining time, reserving 5 minutes for glazing.

3. Combine sugar, corn syrup, mustard, and maple flavoring; blend well. Spread glaze over ham; bake 5 minutes longer.

4. Let stand, wrapped in foil, according to directions.

Makes about 16 servings.

½ bone-in ham butt (3½ to 4 pounds), fully cooked
5 whole cloves
¾ cup light brown sugar
1 cup dark corn syrup
2 tablespoons prepared mustard
1 tablespoon maple flavoring

Microwaved Bacon

Place a double layer of absorbent paper on china platter. Lay bacon strips on paper; cover with a single layer of paper to prevent spattering. Cook as follows:

1 strip	1 minute
2 strips	1 minute, 45 seconds
3 strips	2 minutes, 20 seconds
4 strips	3 minutes

Fruited Ham Loaf

1 tablespoon butter
½ cup dark brown sugar
1 can crushed pineapple
(13½ ounces)
3 maraschino cherries,
quartered
milk
1 egg
1 cup soft bread crumbs
2 tablespoons prepared
mustard
1 teaspoon salt
⅛ teaspoon pepper
1½ pounds fully cooked ham,
ground
½ pound lean pork, ground
2 tablespoons chili sauce

1. Place butter in glass 8-inch square baking pan; heat in microwave oven 1 minute until melted.

2. Stir in sugar.

3. Drain pineapple well; reserve liquid. Spread pineapple evenly over sugar mixture. Arrange cherries on pineapple.

4. Combine pineapple liquid with enough milk to measure 1 cup.

5. In large bowl beat egg slightly with fork. Stir in milk mixture, bread crumbs, mustard, salt and pepper.

6. Add ham and pork; mix thoroughly. Spoon meat mixture evenly over pineapple in baking pan.

7. Thin chili sauce with 1 teaspoon milk; spread evenly on top of meat. Bake 14 minutes.

8. Let stand 10 minutes before serving.

Makes 4 to 6 servings.

Mennonite Ham and Potatoes

1. Pour milk into glass measuring cup; heat in microwave oven 2 minutes; cover top and set aside.

2. Place ham slice in shallow glass baking pan. Arrange potatoes around ham.

3. Combine flour, dry mustard, paprika, and cayenne; mix well. Sprinkle over potatoes and ham. Pour hot milk over all.

4. Cover baking pan top with sheet of waxed paper; do not fold over. Bake 10 minutes; rotate pan and bake 10 minutes longer.

5. Let stand 10 minutes before serving.

Makes 4 to 6 servings.

1 cup milk
1½ to 2 pounds center-cut
  ham slice (1½ inches thick)
2 cans whole white potatoes
  (1 pound each), drained
2 tablespoons flour
1 teaspoon dry mustard
⅛ teaspoon paprika
dash cayenne

New England Ham and Pork Casserole

1. Place butter in 2-quart glass casserole. Heat in microwave oven 1 minute until melted.

2. Stir in flour; blend until smooth. Heat 1 minute.

3. Gradually add chicken stock, then cream, stirring constantly until smooth. Cook 5 minutes, stirring 4 times during cooking period.

4. Add green pepper, mushrooms, ham, pork, salt, and pepper; stir until mixed. Cook, covered, 4 minutes.

5. Let stand 5 minutes before serving.

6. Serve over hot rice, noodles, or waffles.

Makes about 6 servings.

¼ cup butter
¼ cup flour
1 cup chicken stock
1 cup heavy cream
1 medium green pepper,
  cut in thin strips
½ cup sliced mushrooms
2 cups diced cooked ham
2 cups diced cooked pork
¾ teaspoon salt
⅛ teaspoon pepper

81

Chutney-Glazed Ham

1 can fully cooked ham
(5 pounds)
1 cup apple juice
½ cup finely chopped
prepared chutney
½ cup light corn syrup
1 teaspoon lemon juice

1. Remove ham from can; remove gelatin from ham. Place in shallow glass baking pan, fat side down; pour ½ cup apple juice over ham. Bake in microwave oven according to directions on page 74, basting with remaining apple juice every 2 minutes. Remove from oven.

2. Combine chutney, corn syrup, and lemon juice in small measuring glass cup; heat in microwave oven 3 minutes, stirring once.

3. With sharp knife, score ham in diamond pattern. Brush with chutney glaze. Bake 5 minutes longer.

4. Let stand according to directions, wrapped in aluminum foil.

Makes 8 to 10 servings.

Ham and Egg Scallop

3 tablespoons butter
3 tablespoons flour
1½ cups milk
6 hard-cooked eggs
1 cup ground cooked ham
2 tablespoons margarine
½ cup bread crumbs

1. Place butter in glass bowl; heat in microwave oven 1 minute until melted.

2. Stir in flour; blend to a smooth paste; heat 30 seconds.

3. Gradually stir in milk, stirring constantly, until smooth. Heat 2 minutes. Remove from oven; set aside.

4. Chop egg yolks and whites of eggs separately.

5. In shallow 1½-quart glass baking dish, place egg whites in layer; top with ham layer, then with egg yolks.

6. Pour milk sauce over ham and eggs.

7. Place margarine in glass measuring cup; heat 1 minute until melted. Stir in bread crumbs; sprinkle over ham mixture. Cover pan loosely with waxed paper. Bake 10 minutes.

8. Let stand 10 minutes before serving.

Makes 4 servings.

Hawaiian Ham Casserole

1. Place butter in a glass bowl; heat in microwave oven 1 minute until melted. Set aside 1½ tablespoons.

2. Stir flour into remaining 1½ tablespoons butter; blend until smooth.

3. Gradually stir in milk, stirring constantly until blended. Add cheese; heat 1½ minutes, stirring once, until cheese is melted.

4. Lightly butter a shallow glass baking pan; arrange whole bananas in bottom. Brush with remaining melted butter. Spread with mustard.

5. Top with ham. Pour cheese sauce over all. Sprinkle with bread crumbs. Place a sheet of waxed paper loosely on top of pan. Bake 10 to 12 minutes until bananas are tender.

6. Let stand 10 minutes before serving.

Makes 4 servings.

3 tablespoons butter
2½ tablespoons flour
¾ cup milk
1½ cups grated sharp Cheddar cheese
4 ripe but firm bananas, peeled
1 tablespoon prepared mustard
1 cup diced cooked ham
½ cup bread crumbs

Open-Faced Ham Sandwiches

1. Place cheese in glass bowl; stir in milk. Heat in microwave oven 1½ to 2 minutes until cheese is melted.

2. Cut avocado in half; remove seed. Pare, cut into thin lengthwise slices.

3. Place 1 slice of bread on each of 4 individual china plates. Top with a ham slice, then avocado slices. Spoon ¼ of cheese sauce over each serving. Heat in microwave oven as follows:

1 serving	1 minute
2 servings	1 minute, 45 seconds
3 servings	2 minutes, 20 seconds
4 servings	3 minutes

Makes 4 servings

1 cup grated Cheddar cheese
2 tablespoons milk
1 medium avocado, ripe (at room temperature)
4 slices white bread, toasted, buttered
4 slices cooked ham

Poultry

Roasting Chart for Poultry
For Chicken: Based on Fully Thawed, Ready-to-Cook

Weight	Minutes per pound	Directions	Internal temperature taken with meat thermometer after standing time is completed
3 to 5 pounds	6-6½	Place prepared chicken in shallow glass baking pan, breast up. Baste with pan drippings. When ½ time of cooking is completed, turn pan halfway; complete cooking. Let stand 10 minutes.	Insert meat thermometer into center of breast. 180°-185°

For Turkey: Based on Refrigerator Temperature

7 to 15 pounds	6	Place prepared turkey in shallow glass baking pan. Divide total cooking time by 4. Turn turkey 4 times: 1. Breast up 2. On one side 3. On other side 4. Breast down Baste with pan drippings and rotate pan each time turkey is turned. If legs and wings brown too fast before turkey is done, cover with small pieces of thin aluminum foil. Let stand 15 minutes.	Insert meat thermometer into center of breast. 175°-180°

For Other Poultry: Based on Fully Thawed, Ready-to-Cook

Duck: 2½ to 4 pounds	6-6½	Place prepared duck in shallow glass baking pan, breast up. Baste with pan drippings. Pour out	Insert meat thermometer into center of breast. 180°-185°

Wild duck: 2½ to 3 pounds	5-5¼	all excess pan drippings occasionally to avoid sputtering and fatty taste. When ½ time of cooking is completed, turn pan halfway; complete cooking. Let stand 10 minutes.	
Goose: 3 to 5 pounds	6-6½	Proceed as above.	As above.
Cornish Hen: 1 to 1½	4-4½	Place prepared hen in shallow glass baking pan, breast up. Cover breast with 1 slice bacon, cut in half. When ½ of cooking time is completed, remove and discard bacon, turn pan halfway, complete cooking. Let stand 6 minutes.	Insert meat thermometer into center of breast. 180°-185°

Always follow these rules for cooking all poultry:

Chickens may be stuffed. *Do not use* metal skewers to hold stuffing in place. Instead tuck a slice of bread into the cavity.

Turkeys should never be stuffed. Stuffing may be prepared in casserole and cooked separately after standing period of turkey begins.

Tuck legs of poultry into leg band, or tie legs to tail with twine. Tie wings around body.

Do not use salted butter, salted margarine, or salted shortening because the salt toughens the skin and will cause it to split. Use Basting Sauce on page 86.

Lay a sheet of waxed paper across top of bird to prevent spattering oven.

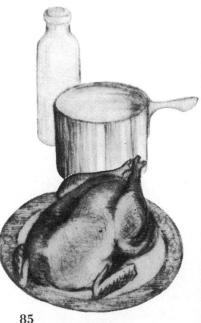

Basting Sauce for Poultry

*1 tablespoon vegetable oil,
or unsalted butter, or
unsalted margarine, or
unsalted shortening
1½ teaspoons paprika
dash cayenne*

1. Place whichever fat you prefer in glass bowl; heat in microwave oven 1 minute.

2. Stir in paprika and cayenne. Brush poultry with mixture.

3. For 7- to 10-pound turkey, double the quantity of the ingredients.

4. For 12- to 15-pound turkey use ¼ cup fat, 2 tablespoons paprika and ⅛ teaspoon cayenne.

Aloha Chicken

*7 tablespoons soy sauce
1 tablespoon Worcestershire
sauce
¼ cup dry white wine
1 clove garlic, minced
2 tablespoons brown sugar
¾ teaspoon ground ginger
dash cayenne
1 chicken fryer (about
2½ pounds), cut up*

1. Combine soy sauce, Worcestershire sauce, wine, garlic, sugar, ginger, and cayenne; mix thoroughly until blended.

2. Place chicken parts in shallow glass pan; pour marinade over chicken and refrigerate 2 hours, turning chicken occasionally to marinate evenly.

3. Arrange chicken parts in shallow baking pan, placing larger pieces in the corners of the pan, and the smaller pieces in the center. Bake in microwave oven 22 to 24 minutes until chicken is tender.

4. Let stand 4 minutes before serving.

Makes 2 servings.

Chicken Divan

*1 package frozen broccoli
spears (10 ounces)
12 thin slices cooked
chicken
1¼ cups Chantilly Sauce
(page 31)
¼ cup grated Parmesan
cheese*

1. Cook frozen broccoli in microwave oven according to directions on page 107. Drain.

2. Arrange cooked broccoli in 2-quart glass casserole; pour ½ Chantilly Sauce over broccoli. Sprinkle with 2 tablespoons cheese.

3. Arrange chicken slices over sauce; pour remaining sauce over chicken. Sprinkle with remaining cheese. Heat in microwave oven, uncovered, 6 to 7 minutes until sauce bubbles.

4. Let stand 1 minute before serving.

Makes 4 servings.

Japanese Chicken Livers

1. If chicken livers are large, cut them in half.

2. Line a shallow glass baking pan with double thickness of absorbent paper.

3. Use 4 *wooden* skewers or wooden chopsticks; thread onions, bacon pieces, water chestnuts, and chicken livers on skewers, ending with an onion.

4. Combine Worcestershire and soy sauce; brush the kabobs generously with the sauce. Place in prepared baking pan (step 2). Cover with single layer of absorbent paper. Bake in microwave oven 8 to 10 minutes until bacon and liver are browned.

Makes 4 servings.

8 chicken livers (about 10 to 12 ounces)
1 can small white onions (8 ounces), drained
2 slices bacon, cut in 12 pieces
1 can water chestnuts (3 ounces), drained
2 tablespoons Worcestershire sauce
1 teaspoon soy sauce.

Streamlined Fried Chicken

1. Wash chicken; dry with absorbent paper.

2. Place crumb coating in shallow dish; mix in paprika and cayenne.

3. Combine egg white with water; beat until blended.

4. Coat each piece of chicken with egg white mixture, then with crumb mixture, or follow package directions of crumb coating. Place chicken in shallow glass baking pan, arranging larger pieces in the corners, and the smaller pieces in the center.

5. Cook in microwave oven 20 minutes until fork tender.

6. Let stand 3 minutes before serving.

7. Serve with Belle Almondine Sauce.

Makes 4 servings.

1 frying chicken (about 2½ to 3 pounds), cut up
1 cup packaged-crumb coating
1 teaspoon paprika
dash cayenne
1 beaten egg white
1 tablespoon water
Belle Almondine Sauce (page 29)

Chicken Mondiale

2 packages frozen asparagus
(10 ounces)
¼ cup butter
¼ cup flour
2 cups chicken broth
½ cup heavy cream
3 tablespoons sherry wine
½ teaspoon salt
⅛ teaspoon pepper
¼ cup grated Parmesan cheese
3 cooked chicken breasts,
thinly sliced
1 tablespoon paprika

1. Cook frozen asparagus in microwave oven according to directions on page 108. Drain.

2. Place butter in glass bowl; heat 1 minute until melted.

3. Add flour; stir until smooth.

4. Gradually stir in chicken, broth, then cream, then wine, stirring constantly until smooth. Cook 5 minutes, stirring after each minute.

5. Add salt and pepper.

6. Place drained asparagus spears in 2-quart glass baking pan. Pour ½ the sauce over them.

7. Add 3 tablespoons cheese to remaining sauce.

8. Place chicken pieces over asparagus; pour remaining sauce over the top. Sprinkle with remaining cheese and paprika. Bake 12 minutes, turning pan halfway after each 4 minutes.

9. Let stand 10 minutes before serving.

Makes 8 servings.

Baked Chicken of the Islands

1 broiler-fryer chicken
(about 3 pounds), cut up
1 teaspoon rosemary
1 teaspoon salt
¼ teaspoon pepper
5 shallots
1 cup unsweetened pineapple
juice
½ teaspoon ginger
¾ teaspoon paprika

1. Wash chicken; pat dry on absorbent paper.

2. Combine rosemary, salt, and pepper; mix well. Rub into chicken. Arrange chicken parts in shallow glass baking pan, placing larger pieces in the corners, and the smaller pieces in the center.

3. Place peeled shallots on top.

4. Combine pineapple juice, and ginger; pour over chicken. Sprinkle with paprika. Cook in microwave oven 20 minutes until tender.

5. Let stand 3 minutes before serving.

Makes 4 servings.

Exotic Chicken a la King

1. Place butter in 2-quart glass casserole; heat in microwave oven 1 minute until melted.

2. Add green pepper, pimientos, and mushrooms; heat 2 minutes, stirring once.

3. Stir in flour and salt; blend until smooth.

4. Gradually stir in chicken broth, then light cream, stirring constantly until well blended.

5. Stir in pepper, turmeric, and sugar. Cook 3 to 4 minutes until sauce is thickened.

6. Blend 2 tablespoons hot sauce into egg yolks; return to sauce and stir. Blend in cream.

7. Add chicken. Cook 5 minutes.

8. Let stand 3 minutes before serving.

9. Serve on toast, biscuits, or hot cooked rice.

Makes 6 servings.

¼ cup butter
½ green pepper, chopped
2 pimientos, chopped
½ cup sliced mushrooms
3 tablespoons flour
½ teaspoon salt
1 cup chicken broth
½ cup light cream
dash pepper
¼ teaspoon powdered turmeric
1 teaspoon sugar
2 slightly beaten egg yolks
½ cup heavy cream
2 cups cubed cooked chicken

Roast Chicken

1. Wash chicken and dry with absorbent paper.

2. Place butter in glass bowl; heat in microwave oven 1 minute, until melted.

3. Add onion; cook 2 minutes, stirring once.

4. Add packaged stuffing; mix well. Lightly fill body cavity of chicken with stuffing; tuck a slice of bread into cavity to hold stuffing in place.

5. Prepare chicken according to directions on page 85. Place in shallow glass baking pan; roast, following directions on page 86, and sprinkle lightly with paprika.

6. Let stand 10 minutes before removing stuffing.

Makes 2 servings.

1 broiler-fryer chicken (about 3 pounds)
¼ cup butter
¼ cup minced onion
1 cup packaged herb-seasoned stuffing
Basting Sauce for poultry (page 86)
paprika

Chicken Salad Almondine

1 tablespoon butter
1 cup thinly sliced celery
½ cup chopped walnuts
½ teaspoon salt
2 teaspoons minced onion
1 cup mayonnaise
2 tablespoons lemon juice
2 cups cooked diced chicken
½ cup grated Cheddar cheese
1 cup crushed potato chips

1. Place butter in glass bowl; heat in microwave oven 30 seconds until melted.

2. Add celery, walnuts, salt, onion; heat 1 minute, stirring once.

3. Combine mayonnaise and lemon juice; add to celery mixture with chicken. Mix thoroughly.

4. Pile lightly into 4 individual glass casseroles. Sprinkle with cheese and potato chips. Place casseroles in a circle in microwave oven. Bake, covered, 4½ to 5 minutes until mixture is heated through.

5. Let stand 2 minutes before serving.

Makes 4 servings.

Scalloped Turkey Siboney

2 tablespoons butter
½ cup water
1½ cups packaged herb-seasoned stuffing
¼ cup minced parsley
1 can cream of chicken soup (10½ ounces)
1 cup leftover turkey gravy
2 cups cubed cooked turkey

1. Place butter and water in glass bowl; heat in microwave oven 1 minute, just until butter is melted.

2. Add stuffing and parsley, tossing lightly until stuffing is evenly moistened; set aside.

3. Pour soup and gravy in glass bowl; stir until blended. Heat 3 minutes, stirring after each minute.

4. In a 2-quart glass baking pan place ½ the turkey in a layer; spoon ½ the gravy mixture. Add ½ the stuffing. Add remaining turkey, ¼ of remaining gravy mixture, and remaining stuffing. Spoon remaining gravy on top. Cook, uncovered, 4½ to 5 minutes until heated through.

5. Let stand 2 minutes before serving.

Makes 4 servings.

Cordon Bleu Duck aux Champignons

1. Pour chicken broth into 2-quart glass casserole; heat in microwave oven to boiling point. Remove from oven.

2. Stir in rice; cover and let stand 5 minutes.

3. Stir in eggs and duckmeat. Spread mushroom soup over top (do not stir or mix). Sprinkle with bread crumbs, then with paprika. Cook in microwave oven 15 minutes, turning casserole halfway every 5 minutes.

4. Let stand 4 minutes before serving.

Makes 6 servings.

3 cups chicken broth
1 cup precooked rice
3 well-beaten eggs
3 cups diced, cooked duck
1 can mushroom soup
(10½ ounces)
1 can whole mushrooms
(3½ ounces), drained
¼ cup bread crumbs
1 teaspoon paprika

Hawaiian Duck

1. Season duck pieces with pepper; place in shallow glass baking dish. Cook in microwave oven 4 minutes.

2. Drain all pan drippings, reserving 1½ tablespoons.

3. Stir in pan drippings, cranberry sauce, water, vinegar, ginger, salt, cloves, and cinnamon; mix well. Pour over duck.

4. Cook 24 minutes longer, turning duck pieces every 8 minutes. Test for doneness. Exact cooking time will depend on age and tenderness of duck.

5. Remove and discard cloves and cinnamon. Let stand 6 minutes before serving.

Makes 4 servings.

1 duck (about 3 pounds),
dressed, cut in quarters
¼ teaspoon pepper
½ cup whole cranberry sauce
2 tablespoons water
2 tablespoons vinegar
dash ginger
¾ teaspoon salt
3 whole cloves
1 stick cinnamon (1 inch)

Fish
and
Shellfish

To cook fish successfully in a microwave oven you only need to follow these simple instructions:

Do not overcook fresh fish as it will lose its moisture and toughen. Cook only until it can be flaked with a fork.

Frozen fish fillets and shellfish may be partially thawed in the microwave oven. Place frozen package on absorbent paper laid in the oven if it is not wrapped in aluminum foil, otherwise you must remove fish from the package. One package of fish fillets (about 1 pound) will thaw sufficiently in about 2 minutes to allow you to separate the pieces. *Do not heat longer,* as this may result in partial cooking of the outer portions. Turn package at least once during thawing.

Directions for thawing shellfish, which vary according to size and shape, are given in each recipe.

Always cook frozen fish shortly after thawing.

Avonshire Stuffed Red Snapper

*1 red snapper (about
1½ pounds), dressed
¼ cup butter
1 teaspoon salt
½ teaspoon onion salt
2 cups day-old bread cubes
2 tablespoons minced onion
1 tablespoon chopped parsley
1 tablespoon chopped celery
½ teaspoon poultry seasoning
¼ cup hot water
¾ teaspoon paprika
4 lemon wedges*

1. Wash fish; wipe dry with absorbent paper.

2. Place butter in glass bowl; heat in microwave oven 1 minute until melted. Brush inside of fish with ½ of melted butter. Sprinkle with salt and onion salt.

3. Combine remaining butter with bread cubes, onion, parsley, celery, poultry seasoning, and water; toss lightly with fork until well mixed.

4. Fill cavity of fish with stuffing; sew sides of fish together with coarse thread. Place fish in shallow glass baking pan, allowing both head and tail to rest in bottom of pan without crowding.

5. Sprinkle fish with paprika. Bake 6½ to 7 minutes or until fish flakes easily.

6. Let stand 5 minutes before serving.

7. Garnish with lemon wedges.

Makes 4 servings.

Fillet of Sole Mornay

*1 package frozen fillet
of flounder (1 pound)
1 tablespoon butter
4 lemon wedges
1¼ cups Mornay Sauce
(page 36)*

1. Place unopened package of fish on absorbent paper, and partially defrost, following directions on page 93, about 1½ minutes. Separate fish; place in shallow glass baking pan.

2. Place butter in glass bowl; heat in microwave oven 30 seconds until melted. Brush fillets with butter. Cook, uncovered, 3½ to 4 minutes or until fish flakes easily. Garnish with lemon wedges. Serve with Mornay Sauce.

Makes 4 servings.

Cod Fillets Floridian

1. Place unopened package of fish on absorbent paper, and partially defrost in microwave oven for 1½ minutes following directions on page 93. Separate fish; place in shallow glass baking pan.

2. Combine lime juice, onions, salt, pepper, ginger, and thyme; mix well. Pour over fish. Dot with butter. Bake 2½ minutes. Turn dish halfway. Bake 2 minutes longer or until fish flakes easily.

3. Serve with lime wedges.

Makes 4 servings.

*1 package frozen cod fillets
 (1 pound)
¼ cup fresh lime juice
2 green onions, thinly sliced
½ teaspoon salt
⅛ teaspoon pepper
¼ teaspoon ground ginger
⅛ teaspoon dried thyme
1 tablespoon butter
4 lime wedges*

New England Poached Codfish

1. Place fish in single layer in shallow glass baking pan.

2. Pour water over fish. Add onion, bay leaf, allspice, ¾ teaspoon salt, and pepper. Heat in microwave oven 3 minutes.

3. Cover baking pan with plastic film, punctured in center to allow steam to escape. Cook 4 minutes longer, or until fish flakes easily.

4. Transfer fish onto platter. Drain liquid; reserve.

5. Place butter in glass bowl; heat 30 seconds until melted.

6. Stir in flour; blend to a smooth paste. Stir in remaining salt.

7. Gradually stir in fish liquid, stirring constantly until smooth. Heat 1½ minutes. Add mustard and lemon juice. Heat 1 minute longer, stirring twice.

8. Spoon sauce over fish.

Makes about 6 servings.

*2½ pounds fresh codfish
 steaks
1¼ cups water
1 medium onion, sliced
1 bay leaf
dash allspice
1 teaspoon salt
¼ teaspoon pepper
2 tablespoons butter
2 tablespoons flour
¼ cup prepared
 mustard
1 tablespoon lemon juice*

Pacific Poached Salmon Steaks

*4 fresh salmon steaks
(about 2 pounds)
2 cups water
3 tablespoons vinegar
2 tablespoons lemon juice
½ sliced lemon
½ small onion, sliced
6 whole cloves
1 bay leaf
1 stalk celery, cut into
pieces
3 sprigs parsley
1¼ teaspoons salt
Soubise Sauce (page 39)*

1. Wash fish; pat dry with absorbent paper.

2. Combine water, vinegar, lemon juice, lemon, onion, cloves, bay leaf, celery, parsley, and salt in glass bowl; heat, uncovered, in microwave oven 5 minutes.

3. Arrange fish in single layer in shallow glass baking pan; pour hot liquid over fish. Cook, uncovered, 5 minutes or until fish flakes easily.

4. Allow fish to cool in stock.

5. Serve cold with Soubise Sauce.

Makes 4 servings.

Fillet of Sole Clementine

*1 package frozen fillet of
sole (1 pound)
½ teaspoon salt
1 can frozen oyster stew
(10 ounces)
¼ cup canned sliced mushrooms
1 teaspoon chopped pimiento
1 teaspoon celery salt
2 tablespoons lemon juice*

1. Place unopened package of fish on absorbent paper, and partially defrost in microwave oven for 1½ minutes following directions on page 93. Separate fish; place in shallow glass baking pan. Sprinkle with salt.

2. Open both ends of oyster stew can; push frozen stew out into a 1-quart glass casserole. Heat, covered, 3 minutes, stirring twice, until thawed.

3. Add mushrooms, and pimiento; stir until blended. Pour over fish. Sprinkle with celery salt. Cook 4 minutes. Turn baking pan halfway. Cook 2 minutes longer, or until fish flakes easily. Sprinkle with lemon juice.

Makes 4 servings.

Fillets of Flounder Florentine

1. Place unopened package of fish on absorbent paper, and partially defrost in microwave oven for 1½ minutes, following directions on page 93. Separate fish; place in shallow baking pan. Sprinkle with lemon juice.

2. Add garlic, onion, mushrooms, tarragon, and wine. Cook 4½ minutes or until fish flakes easily with fork; do not overcook.

3. Cook frozen spinach in microwave oven according to directions on page 108. Drain well; pat lightly between absorbent paper. Add ½ teaspoon salt, ⅛ teaspoon pepper, and 2 tablespoons cream; mix well. Place spinach mixture in another shallow baking pan, making an even layer.

4. Carefully remove fish from baking pan; reserve liquid. Drain fish well. Arrange on spinach in single layer.

5. Place butter in 1½-quart glass casserole; heat 30 seconds until melted.

6. Stir in flour; blend to a smooth paste.

7. Measure reserved liquid to ¾ cup; stir into flour mixture, stirring constantly until well blended. Add vegetables from fish pan, remaining ¼ teaspoon salt, ⅛ teaspoon pepper, and light cream; heat 3 minutes, stirring twice until sauce is bubbly. Strain; discard vegetables.

8. Spoon sauce over fish and spinach; heat, uncovered, 2 minutes. Spoon Hollandaise Sauce and serve.

Makes 4 servings.

1 package frozen flounder
fillets (1 pound)
1 tablespoon lemon juice
1 small clove garlic, minced
1 green onion, minced
3 tablespoons chopped
mushrooms
2 teaspoons dried tarragon
½ cup Sauterne wine
1 package frozen chopped
spinach (10 ounces)
¾ teaspoon salt
¼ teaspoon pepper
½ cup heavy cream
2 tablespoons butter
2 tablespoons flour
¼ cup light cream
Hollandaise Sauce
(page 34)

Halibut Nagasaki

1. Combine wine, soy and Worcestershire sauces, sugar, garlic powder, oil, onion, and celery in glass bowl; mix well. Heat in microwave oven 1 minute stirring once.

2. Arrange fish in single layer in shallow glass baking pan; pour soy sauce mixture. Let stand 10 minutes.

3. Turn fish over. Cover pan with plastic film. Cook in microwave oven 4 minutes, rotating pan once.

Makes 4 servings.

¼ cup dry white wine
3 tablespoons soy sauce
1 tablespoon Worcestershire
sauce
2 teaspoons sugar
⅛ teaspoon garlic powder
1½ tablespoons vegetable oil
1 tablespoon minced onion
1 teaspoon minced celery
4 halibut fillets
(about 1½ pounds)

Perch Fillets Cantonese

1 package frozen perch
fillets (1 pound)
2 tablespoons vegetable oil
2 teaspoons soy sauce
dash Tabasco
½ teaspoon ground ginger
2 tablespoons brown sugar
2 tablespoons chopped parsley
4 lime wedges

1. Place unopened package of fish on absorbent paper, and partially defrost in microwave oven for 1½ minutes following directions on page 93.

2. Place fish in glass dish.

3. Combine oil, soy sauce, Tabasco, ginger, and brown sugar; mix well. Pour over fish. Let stand in refrigerator 4 hours.

4. Remove fish from marinade to a shallow glass baking pan. Cook, uncovered, 3½ to 4 minutes or until fish flakes easily with fork.

5. Just before serving, sprinkle with parsley and garnish with lime wedges.

Makes 4 servings.

Stuffed Salmon Columbia

2 tablespoons butter
½ cup minced celery
½ small onion, minced
¼ cup canned sliced
mushrooms
⅛ teaspoon thyme
¾ teaspoon salt
⅛ teaspoon pepper
1 teaspoon grated lemon peel
3 tablespoons lemon juice
½ cup water
¾ cup packaged precooked
rice
1 piece fresh salmon (about
3 pounds), dressed
4 slices bacon
Elegant Parsley Sauce
(page 32)

1. Place 1 tablespoon butter in 1-quart glass casserole; heat in microwave oven 30 seconds until melted.

2. Add celery, onion, and mushrooms; heat 3 minutes, stirring twice.

3. Add thyme, salt, pepper, lemon peel and juice, and water; heat 4 minutes longer until liquid is bubbly.

4. Add rice; cover, and let stand 5 minutes until liquid is absorbed.

5. Fill cavity of fish with stuffing; skewer with wooden picks.

6. Place remaining butter in shallow glass baking pan; heat 30 seconds until melted. Place stuffed fish in pan. Cover top with waxed paper. Bake 8 minutes.

7. Carefully turn fish over; place bacon

slices on top. Cover pan with waxed paper; bake 5 to 6 minutes longer or until fish flakes easily in the center.

8. Remove wooden picks. Serve fish with Elegant Parsley Sauce.

Makes 6 to 8 servings.

California Salmon Loaf

1. Drain salmon; flake and remove bones.

2. Add egg, bread crumbs, cream, celery, parsley, salt, cayenne, onion, and lemon juice; mix well. Spoon mixture evenly into 8-inch glass pie plate. Lay a sheet of waxed paper on top. Cook in microwave oven 8 minutes.

3. Let stand 5 minutes before serving.

4. To serve, cut into pie wedges, spoon Broccoli-Cheese Sauce over the top.

Makes 4 servings.

1 can salmon (1 pound)
1 slightly beaten egg
¾ cup soft bread crumbs
¼ cup heavy cream
¼ cup chopped celery
¼ cup chopped parsley
¼ teaspoon salt
dash cayenne
1 tablespoon minced onion
2 teaspoons lemon juice
Broccoli-Cheese Sauce
(page 30)

Madras Tuna Casserole

1. Place macaroni and 2½ teaspoons salt in covered 2-quart glass casserole.

2. Add water; heat in microwave oven 8 to 10 minutes, stirring once. Remove from oven; drain.

3. In same casserole, drain tuna fish liquid; add onion, olives, parsley, remaining salt, curry powder, and pepper. Stir to blend; heat 65 seconds. Add soup and cooked macaroni; mix well.

4. Top with buttered bread crumbs. Heat 6 minutes.

Makes 4 to 6 servings.

2 cups elbow macaroni
1 tablespoon salt
2 cups water
2 cans tuna fish
(3½ ounces each)
2 tablespoons minced onion
½ cup sliced ripe olives
2 tablespoons chopped parsley
1½ teaspoons curry powder
⅛ teaspoon pepper
1 can cream of celery soup
(10½ ounces)
½ cup buttered bread crumbs

Hankow Creamed Tuna

2 tablespoons butter
½ cup finely chopped celery
1 tablespoon minced parsley
2 tablespoons flour
¼ teaspoon salt
⅛ teaspoon cayenne
½ teaspoon Worcestershire
sauce
½ teaspoon onion salt
¾ cup milk
¼ cup light cream
1 can tuna (7 ounces)
1 teaspoon lemon juice
1 can Chinese noodles
(3 ounces) (vermicelli-type)

1. Place butter in 1½-quart glass casserole; heat in microwave oven 1 minute until melted.

2. Add celery; cook 1 minute. Blend in parsley, flour, salt, cayenne, Worcestershire sauce, and onion salt.

3. Gradually stir in milk then cream, stirring constantly until blended. Cook 4 minutes, stirring at the end of each minute.

4. Drain tuna; flake with a fork. Stir into sauce with lemon juice; heat 1½ minutes longer.

5. Serve over Chinese noodles.

Makes 4 cups.

Party Tuna Loaves

6 tablespoons butter
1 cup chopped onion
1 cup chopped celery
3 tablespoons minced parsley
1 cup dry bread crumbs
2 hard-cooked eggs,
chopped
⅔ cup heavy cream
3 tablespoons lemon juice
2 well-beaten eggs
1 teaspoon salt
¼ teaspoon pepper
dash marjoram
3 cans tuna (7 ounces each),
drained, flaked
Pacific Fish Sauce
(page 37)

1. Place ¼ cup butter in glass bowl; heat in microwave oven 1 minute until melted.

2. Add onion, celery, and parsley; cook 3 minutes.

3. Add ¾ cup bread crumbs, eggs, cream, lemon juice, beaten eggs, salt, pepper, marjoram, and tuna; mix thoroughly.

4. Divide tuna mixture equally among eight 6-ounce glass custard cups.

5. Brush top with remaining 2 tablespoons butter which has been melted; sprinkle with remaining bread crumbs.

6. Place cups in a circle in microwave oven; heat 12 to 14 minutes until heated through.

7. Serve with Pacific Fish Sauce.

Makes 8 servings.

Lobster-Tails Bon Vivant

1. Remove wrapping from each lobster-tail; place in shallow glass baking pan. Heat in microwave oven 2½ minutes. Let stand at room temperature 5 to 10 minutes until thoroughly thawed.

2. With kitchen shears cut lengthwise down the back and through the hard shell; press tail open flat. Turn meat side up in pan.

3. Place butter in glass bowl; heat in microwave oven 1 minute until melted. Stir in lemon juice. Brush lobster-tails generously with butter mixture. Cook 2 to 2½ minutes being careful not to overcook. Remove as soon as lobster meat loses its transparent color.

1 package frozen lobster-tails (10 ounces)
3 tablespoons butter
2 teaspoons lemon juice

Makes 2 servings.

Lobster d'Argent

1. Cook each lobster separately; place 1 lobster in 2½-quart glass casserole.

2. Pour 3 cups boiling water over lobster; cook, covered, in microwave oven 5 minutes, turning lobster twice. Remove from water.

3. Combine celery soup and cream; mix well.

4. Place butter in glass bowl; heat 1 minute until melted. Add soup mixture, cheese, parsley, salt, pepper, mustard, horseradish, and egg yolk; stir until well blended. Heat 4 minutes, stirring once.

5. Split cooked lobsters lengthwise; remove stomachs and intestinal veins; crack claws. Remove tail meat; cut into small pieces. Place cut tail meat back in tail shells. Place lobster on shallow baking dish, split side up. Pour celery sauce into body cavities and over tail meat. Sprinkle with bread crumbs; dot with butter. Heat 1½ minutes for 1 lobster or 2½ minutes for 2 lobsters.

2 lobsters (about 1½
  pounds each)
boiling salted water
1 can cream of celery
  soup (10½ ounces)
2 tablespoons heavy cream
1 tablespoon butter
1 tablespoon grated Swiss
  cheese
1 tablespoon chopped parsley
½ teaspoon salt
pinch pepper
pinch dry mustard
½ teaspoon horseradish
1 beaten egg yolk
¼ cup fine bread crumbs
2 tablespoons margarine

Makes 2 servings.

101

Lobster Newburg

¼ cup butter
3 tablespoons flour
2 cups light cream
(1 pint)
1 well-beaten egg
1 teaspoon salt
2 tablespoons sherry wine
2 packages frozen lobster-
tails (10 ounces each)

1. Place butter in 1½-quart glass baking dish; heat in microwave oven 65 seconds until melted.

2. Stir in flour; heat 35 seconds.

3. Add cream; cook 4 minutes until thickened, stirring once.

4. Add a little of hot mixture to egg; blend egg into sauce. Add salt and wine.

5. Cook lobster-tails in microwave oven according to directions on page 93. Remove from shell; cut into pieces.

6. Add lobster to hot sauce; heat 2 minutes until bubbly. Serve over hot buttered toast or rice.

Makes 4 servings.

Shrimp Marinara

1 package frozen shrimp
(10 ounces), uncooked
¼ cup hot water
2 teaspoons lemon juice
¼ teaspoon salt
¼ teaspoon seafood
seasoning
2 tablespoons olive oil
1 clove garlic, minced
1 teaspoon chopped parsley
dash cayenne
⅓ cup dry white wine
1 medium tomato, peeled,
chopped
½ teaspoon onion salt

1. Place frozen shrimp in 2-quart glass casserole; heat in microwave oven 2 minutes, 15 seconds. Separate shrimp.

2. Remove shells and devein shrimp. Place cleaned shrimp in casserole.

3. Combine hot water, lemon juice, salt, and seafood seasoning; pour over shrimp. Cook, uncovered, 4 minutes. Drain shrimp; set aside.

4. Pour oil into casserole; heat 1 minute. Add garlic, parsley, and cayenne; cook 1 minute, stirring once.

5. Add wine, tomato, and onion salt; mix well. Cook, covered, 3 minutes.

6. Add shrimp; heat 2 minutes.

7. Serve over hot cooked rice or hot buttered noodles.

Makes 4 servings.

102

Bayou Shrimp Creole

1. Place butter in 2½-quart glass casserole; heat in microwave oven 1 minute until melted.

2. Add green pepper, onion, celery, and parsley; cook 3½ minutes or until vegetables are crisp-tender, stirring vegetables twice.

3. Sprinkle flour over vegetables; stir until blended.

4. Add tomatoes; cook, uncovered, 3 minutes. Stir; cook 3 minutes longer.

5. Add sugar, Tabasco, thyme, salt, and pepper; stir to blend.

6. Add shrimp; cook, covered, 6 minutes, stirring 3 times.

7. Let stand 5 minutes. Serve over rice.

Makes 4 servings.

2 tablespoons butter
¾ cup chopped green pepper
1 cup chopped onion
¾ cup chopped celery
¼ cup chopped parsley
1½ tablespoons flour
1 can tomatoes (14½ ounces)
1 teaspoon sugar
5 drops Tabasco
dash thyme
1 teaspoon salt
⅛ teaspoon white pepper
1 pound raw shrimp, shelled, cleaned
2 cups hot cooked rice

Scallops Indienne

1. Place frozen scallops in 2-quart glass casserole; heat in microwave oven 2 minutes 15 seconds. Separate scallops. Wash in cold water; drain.

2. Place butter in 1½-quart glass casserole; heat 1 minute until melted.

3. Add shallots and scallops; cook 4 minutes, stirring twice.

4. Combine cornstarch, curry powder, and salt; pour 2 tablespoons liquid from scallop casserole. Blend to a smooth paste. Add to scallops, stirring to blend. Cook 2 minutes.

5. Add cooked rice and 1 or 2 tablespoons water, if necessary. Toss lightly; heat 30 seconds.

Makes 4 servings.

1 package frozen scallops (1 pound)
1 tablespoon butter
¼ cup sliced shallots
1½ teaspoons cornstarch
1¾ teaspoons curry powder
¼ teaspoon salt
2 cups hot cooked rice
water

103

Pioneer Oyster Fry

4 slices bacon
12 medium oysters, drained
½ cup flour
1 slightly beaten egg
½ cup fine dry bread crumbs
1 tablespoon butter
4 eggs
½ teaspoon salt
¼ teaspoon white pepper
dash cayenne

1. Cook bacon in microwave oven according to instructions on page 80. Cut in half; set aside.

2. Dip each oyster into flour, then into slightly beaten egg, then into bread crumbs until evenly coated.

3. Place butter in 9-inch glass pie plate; heat in microwave oven 1 minute until melted and bubbly.

4. Arrange oysters in single layer in butter. Cook 2 minutes, turning oysters over once.

5. Beat eggs with salt, pepper, and cayenne; pour over oysters. Cook 5 minutes until eggs are almost set in center. Top with cooked bacon; heat 40 seconds longer.

6. To serve, cut into wedges.

Makes 4 servings.

Crab Angélique

1 package frozen chopped spinach (10 ounces)
3 tablespoons butter
2 tablespoons flour
½ teaspoon salt
dash pepper
1 cup milk
½ cup light cream
½ cup heavy cream
1 cup grated Swiss cheese
1 tablespoon lemon juice
2 cans crabmeat (6½ ounces each), drained, flaked
¼ cup dry bread crumbs
1 teaspoon paprika

1. Cook spinach in microwave oven according to directions on page 108. Drain well. Place in 1½-quart glass casserole.

2. Place butter in glass bowl; heat 1 minute until melted.

3. Stir in flour, salt, and pepper; blend to a smooth paste. Heat 1 minute.

4. Gradually add milk, then light cream, then heavy cream, stirring constantly, until blended and smooth. Heat 3 minutes, stirring twice.

5. Add cheese; stir until melted.

6. Add lemon juice and crabmeat; mix well. Pour over spinach. Sprinkle with bread crumbs and paprika. Cook 5 minutes.

7. Let stand 5 minutes before serving.

Makes 4 servings.

Vegetables

Both fresh and frozen vegetables benefit greatly from microwave cooking. Color and flavor are retained to a much greater degree than in conventional cooking and, in the case of fresh vegetables, care should be applied to cook them crisp-tender. Then they will be garden-fresh and delicious.

If, however, this degree of doneness does not suit you, and you prefer your vegetables more well-done, then be careful not to overcook them because they become dehydrated and tough.

Seasoning should not be sprinkled on top of the vegetables as this tends to dehydrate them. Instead, sprinkle the desired amount of salt or other seasonings in the bottom of the utensil.

Vegetables cook more evenly and faster when they are covered. Stir vegetables at least once during cooking time. Vegetables with skins, such as potatoes, are easy and quick to bake in the microwave oven; leave a space of about 1 inch between them, prick them with a fork, and turn them once or twice during cooking.

Vegetables cooked electronically will continue to cook after they are removed from the oven; allow them to stand, covered, a few minutes before serving.

Cooking Chart for Fresh Vegetables

Vegetable	Amount	Cooking Instructions	Time in Minutes
Artichokes	2 large	See special instructions in recipe, page 109.	
Asparagus	1 pound	In 2 tablespoons to ¼ cup water, depending on size.	6-8
Beans, green or waxed	1 pound	In ¼ cup water.	8
Beans, lima	1 pound	In ½ cup water.	7
Broccoli	3 spears	In ¼ cup water.	9
Cabbage	1 small	Shredded, in about 4 cups, 2 tablespoons hot water.	7-8
Carrots	2 cups	Cut in 1-inch pieces, in ¼ cup water.	7
Cauliflower	1 head (1 pound)	Cut into flowerets, in 2 tablespoons water.	5
	1 head	Whole, in ¼ cup water.	10
Corn, cut	2 ears	In ¼ cup water.	5
Corn on the cob	2 ears	Buttered and seasoned, in husks.	3-4
Okra	1 pound	In ¼ cup water.	7
Onions	1 pound	Medium-size, whole, in ½ cup water.	7
Parsnips	1 pound	Peeled, sliced, in ½ cup water.	8
Peas	1 pound	Shelled, in ¼ cup water.	4
Potatoes	varied	See special instructions on pages 114-117.	
Rutabaga	1 pound	Peeled, cubed, in 3 cups, 1/3 cup water.	10
Spinach	½ pound	In 2 tablespoons water.	3-4
Squash			
Acorn	1 pound	Halve and remove seeds.	8
Butternut	1 pound	See special instructions on page 118.	
Summer	1 pound	See special instructions on page 118.	
Turnips, fresh	1 bunch	Peeled, cubed, in ¼ cup water.	10
Yams	2 pounds	In ¼ cup water.	12
Zucchini	1 pound	In 2 tablespoons water.	7

Use a 1½-quart glass casserole, with cover.

Place seasoning in bottom of casserole before adding vegetables and water.

108

NOTE: Canned vegetables are already cooked and require only heating. Turn contents of can into glass casserole, add seasonings if desired, stir lightly, and heat 1½ to 5 minutes depending on quantity and kind of vegetable.

For Frozen Vegetable Chart see frozen food section, Frozen Assets, page 192.

Artichokes Mousseline

1. Wash artichokes by placing them in cold water to cover; let stand 5 minutes. Place in fresh water; let stand 5 minutes longer. Drain.

2. Slice off ⅓ of upper tip of each artichoke, trim and cut off thorny ends of tips of lower leaves. Peel off small leaves around the base and cut off stem evenly.

3. Combine 1 quart water with 3 tablespoons vinegar; add prepared artichokes and let stand until ready to cook. Drain thoroughly.

4. Pour 1 cup water in 1½-quart glass casserole; add oil and lemon juice; stir until blended. Cook, uncovered, 3½ minutes in microwave oven until mixture boils.

5. Add prepared and drained artichokes. Cook, covered, 9 minutes, turning artichokes over after each 3 minutes of cooking until bases are tender when pierced with fork and lower leaves pull away easily.

6. Let stand, covered, 2 minutes. Drain artichokes well. Serve hot or cold with Mousseline Sauce.

Makes 2 servings.

2 large artichokes
(about 4 inches)
water
3 tablespoons vinegar
1 teaspoon vegetable oil
1 tablespoon lemon juice
Mousseline Sauce
(page 36)

To Double the Recipe

Use 4 artichokes, place in 2½-quart glass casserole. Increase cooking water to 1½ cups and lemon juice to 1½ tablespoons. Do not increase oil. Increase cooking time to 15 minutes.

109

Asparagus Hollandaise

1 pound fresh asparagus
2 tablespoons water
¾ teaspoon salt
⅛ teaspoon white pepper
Mock Hollandaise Sauce
(page 35)

1. Clean asparagus; place in a 1½-quart oblong glass baking pan.

2. Add water. Cover top of pan with un-punctured plastic film. Cook in microwave oven 6 minutes, turning asparagus over twice during cooking time.

3. Remove from oven; season with salt and pepper. Let stand 2 minutes. Drain.

4. Serve with Mock Hollandaise Sauce.

Makes 4 servings.

Green Beans Lyonnaise

1 pound fresh green beans
¼ cup water
1 tablespoon butter
1 tablespoon chopped onion
dash cloves
Bechamel Sauce (page 28)
4 pimiento strips

1. Wash beans; drain. Trim ends; cut lengthwise into slivers. Place in 1½-quart glass casserole; heat in microwave oven, covered, 8 minutes or until crisp-tender. Let stand 2 minutes; drain.

2. Place butter in glass bowl; heat 30 seconds until melted.

3. Add onion, cook 2 minutes. Stir in Béchamel Sauce, and cloves; mix well. Stir into drained beans.

4. Before serving, garnish top with pimiento strips.

Makes 4 servings.

Wax Beans a la Ramona

1 pound fresh wax beans
¼ cup water
¾ teaspoon salt
teaspoon white pepper
Beef Sauce Ramona
(page 29)

1. Wash beans; drain. Cut into 1½-inch pieces. Place in 2-quart glass casserole.

2. Pour water over beans; cook, covered, in microwave oven 8 minutes, stirring every 2 minutes.

3. Let stand 1 minute; drain. Season with salt and pepper.

4. Serve with Beef Sauce Ramona spooned over them.

Makes 4 servings.

Lima Beans Romanoff

1. Cover beans with cold water; refrigerate, covered, overnight.

2. Drain beans. Turn into a 2-quart glass casserole; add ½ cup water. Cook, covered, in microwave oven 7 minutes, stirring 3 times during cooking. Drain.

3. Place butter in glass bowl; heat 1 minute until melted. Add onions, and mushrooms; heat 3 minutes, stirring twice.

4. Add flour, paprika, and salt; stir until well blended. Heat 1 minute. Add mixture to drained beans; stir until blended. Heat 1 minute. Stir in sour cream; heat 1 minute longer.

5. Let stand 2 minutes before serving. Sprinkle with parsley.

Makes about 6 servings.

1 pound dried lima beans
water
¼ cup butter
¾ cup finely chopped onions
½ pound fresh mushrooms,
  thinly sliced
1 tablespoon flour
2 teaspoons paprika
1 teaspoon salt
2 cups sour cream
2 tablespoons chopped parsley

New England Baked Beans

1. Cook bacon according to directions on page 80. Crumble; set aside.

2. Combine beans, onion, ketchup, chili sauce, and mustard in 1½-quart glass casserole. Mix thoroughly.

3. Sprinkle bacon on top. Cook, uncovered, in microwave oven, 5 minutes.

4. Let stand 2 minutes before serving.

Makes 2 servings.

1 strip bacon
1 can baked beans
  (1 pound)
2 tablespoons minced onion
2 tablespoons ketchup
1 teaspoon chili sauce
1 teaspoon prepared mustard

111

Broccoli Italiano

3-4 broccoli stalks
(about 1 pound)
¼ cup water
2 tablespoons butter
½ cup sliced green onions
2 canned pimientos,
chopped
1 teaspoon grated lemon peel
2 tablespoons lemon juice
¾ teaspoon salt
⅛ teaspoon pepper

1. Discard large leaves and tough portions of broccoli stalks. Wash thoroughly; drain. Split each stalk lengthwise into halves. Place in 1½-quart glass casserole; pour water over broccoli. Cook, covered, in microwave oven 9 minutes or until crisp-tender and green color becomes vivid. Drain.

2. Place butter in glass bowl; heat 30 seconds until melted.

3. Add onions; cook 2 minutes, stirring twice.

4. Add pimientos, lemon peel and juice, salt, and pepper; stir to blend.

5. Arrange broccoli in serving plate; pour pimiento mixture over top.

Makes 4 servings.

Irish Cabbage

1 small head cabbage (about
4 cups), shredded
¾ teaspoon salt
⅛ teaspoon pepper
2 tablespoons hot water
Mustard Cream Sauce
(page 37)

1. Place shredded cabbage, salt, and pepper in 2-quart glass casserole.

2. Pour water over top; stir. Cook, covered, in microwave oven 7 to 8 minutes, stirring once. Drain.

3. Turn cabbage onto serving plate; spoon Mustard Cream Sauce on top.

Makes 4 servings.

Maine Glazed Carrots

2 tablespoons butter
¼ cup light brown sugar
¼ cup cranberry-orange
relish
1 tablespoon brandy
2-½ cups sliced cooked
carrots

1. Place butter in glass serving dish; heat in microwave oven 50 seconds until melted.

2. Add brown sugar, relish, and brandy; stir until well blended.

3. Add carrots; heat in oven 70 seconds or until thoroughly heated, turning them over once.

Makes 4 servings.

Buttered Carrots Alsacienne

1. Pare and slice carrots to ¼ inch to yield 2½ cups.

2. Place in 1½-quart glass casserole. Add onion, celery, salt, butter, water, and lemon juice. Cook, covered, in microwave oven 10 to 12 minutes, stirring twice during cooking.

3. Stir in parsley. Let stand 2 minutes.

Makes 4 servings.

1 bunch fresh carrots
1 tablespoon minced onion
1 tablespoon minced celery
¼ teaspoon salt
1 tablespoon butter
¼ cup hot water
½ teaspoon lemon juice
2 tablespoons chopped parsley

Cauliflower Frankel

1. Clean cauliflower and cut into flowerets. Place in 1½-quart glass casserole.

2. Add water; cook, covered, in microwave oven 5 minutes. Drain. Season with salt and pepper.

3. Let stand 1 minute. Serve with Mushroom Cheese Sauce.

Makes 4 servings.

1 cauliflower (about 1 pound)
2 tablespoons water
¾ teaspoon salt
⅛ teaspoon white pepper
Mushroom Cheese Sauce (page 36)

Deviled Cauliflower

1. Clean head of cauliflower and leave whole. Place in 2-quart glass casserole.

2. Pour water over cauliflower; cook, covered, in microwave oven 10 minutes, turning casserole halfway once.

3. Drain; season with salt and pepper.

4. Let stand 1 minute. Turn into serving platter. Spoon Deviled Ham Sauce over top.

Makes 4 servings.

1 cauliflower (about 1 pound)
¼ cup water
¾ teaspoon salt
⅛ teaspoon pepper
Deviled Ham Sauce (page 31)

Supreme Corn-on-the-Cob

4 ears fresh sweet corn
melted butter
salt

1. Pull outer husks off ears of corn leaving only the inner husk intact. Carefully pull back inner husks; remove silk.

2. Brush ears of corn with melted butter and season with salt. Replace husks; secure with string tied on tip of each ear.

3. Lay corn in an oblong glass baking pan. Cook in microwave oven 3 minutes. Roll corn over; cook 3 minutes longer.

4. Remove string. Allow husks to remain around ears of corn until ready to eat.

Makes 4 servings.

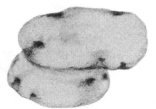

Baked Potatoes

Select potatoes of uniform shape and size, about 7 ounces each. Scrub them well. Prick each potato all the way through with a metal skewer or an ice pick. Arrange potatoes on absorbent paper in microwave oven, in a circle when cooking more than 2, leaving about a 1-inch space between them.

Bake approximately as indicated below, checking for doneness, as cooking time varies according to variety and size. Halfway through cooking time turn potatoes over.

1 potato	4 minutes
2 potatoes	7- 8 minutes
4 potatoes	14-16 minutes

114

Baked Sweet Potatoes

Select sweet potatoes for uniform shape and size, about 7 or 8 ounces each. Scrub the potatoes well. Prick each potato all the way through with a metal skewer or an ice pick. Arrange them on absorbent paper in microwave oven in a circle, when cooking more than 2, leaving about a 1-inch space between them.

Bake approximately as indicated below, checking for doneness as cooking time varies according to variety and size. Halfway through cooking time turn potatoes over.

1 sweet potato	3½ minutes
2 sweet potatoes	7 minutes
4 sweet potatoes	15 minutes

Baked Potatoes Paprikash

1. Bake potatoes according to directions on page 114. Let stand 10 minutes.

2. Cut a thin oval slice through skin from the top of each potato. Scoop out potato, leaving the skin intact, to form a boat.

3. Mash potato; add butter, milk, cream, salt, and pepper. Whip until potato mixture is light and fluffy. Lightly spoon mixture back into potato shells.

4. Top each potato with 1 tablespoon cheese; sprinkle with paprika.

5. Place potatoes on absorbent paper and heat in microwave oven 4 minutes.

Makes 4 servings.

*4 uniform baking potatoes
  (about 7 ounces each)
2 tablespoons butter
½ cup milk
¼ cup light cream
1-¾ teaspoons salt
¼ teaspoon pepper
½ cup sharp Cheddar cheese,
  grated
1 teaspoon paprika*

115

Escalloped Potatoes Sharyl

4 medium potatoes, pared,
sliced ⅛ inch thick
3 tablespoons flour
¾ teaspoon salt
⅛ teaspoon white pepper
1 cup scalded milk
2 tablespoons butter
½ teaspoon paprika

1. Arrange ½ of sliced potatoes in 1¼-quart glass baking pan.

2. Combine flour, salt, and pepper; sprinkle ½ of mixture over potatoes.

3. Arrange remaining potatoes on top; sprinkle with remaining flour mixture.

4. Pour milk over potatoes; do not stir. Dot with butter and sprinkle with paprika. Cook in microwave oven 11 to 12 minutes or until potatoes are tender.

Makes 4 servings.

Potatoes au Gratin

4 medium potatoes, pared,
sliced ⅛ inch thick
3 tablespoons flour
¾ teaspoon salt
⅛ teaspoon celery salt
1 cup grated Cheddar cheese
¾ cup scalded milk
¼ cup scalded light cream
2 tablespoons butter
½ teaspoon paprika

1. Arrange ½ of sliced potatoes in 1¼-quart glass baking pan.

2. Combine flour, salt, celery salt, and cheese; mix well. Sprinkle ½ of mixture over potatoes.

3. Arrange remaining potatoes on top; sprinkle with remaining flour mixture.

4. Combine milk and cream; pour over potatoes. Do not stir. Dot with butter and sprinkle with paprika. Cook in microwave oven 12 to 13 minutes or until potatoes are tender.

Makes 4 servings.

To Scald Milk or Cream

Place in glass measuring cup; heat in microwave oven 1½ to 2½ minutes depending on quantity.

Potatoes Chantilly

1. Prepare potatoes according to package directions; place in greased shallow glass baking dish.

2. Whip cream; fold in cheese. Season with salt and pepper. Spread over potatoes.

3. Heat in microwave oven 4 minutes. Serve immediately.

Makes 4 servings.

1 envelope instant mashed potatoes
½ cup heavy cream
¼ cup grated sharp Cheddar cheese
¾ teaspoon salt
⅛ teaspoon pepper

Pierre's Sweet Potatoes

1. Wash and dry oranges; cut in half. Scoop out center and squeeze juice. Measure to ¾ cup and reserve.

2. Remove membrane from shells and, if desired, snip edges with scissors to form scalloped design. Set aside.

3. Bake sweet potatoes according to directions on page 115. Peel hot potatoes. Combine with butter, ¼ cup brown sugar, and salt; whip until light and fluffy, gradually adding reserved orange juice. Fill orange shells with mixture.

4. Place filled shells in shallow glass baking dish. Combine remaining 2 tablespoons brown sugar with corn syrup and allspice; blend well. Spoon some of the mixture on top of each shell. Bake in microwave oven 5 minutes.

Makes 6 servings.

3 large oranges
4 sweet potatoes (about 2 pounds)
4 teaspoons butter
6 tablespoons brown sugar
½ teaspoon salt
1 teaspoon dark corn syrup
allspice

Honey-Spiced Acorn Squash

1 acorn squash (about 1 to
1½ pounds)
4 teaspoons butter
¼ teaspoon salt
¼ teaspoon ginger
⅛ teaspoon cinnamon
1 tablespoon honey

1. Scrub squash. Leave whole. Pierce with metal skewer right through in several places. Place on paper plate; bake in microwave oven 4 minutes. Turn over; bake 4 minutes longer. Let stand 3 minutes.

2. Cut squash in half lengthwise; remove seeds and stringy fibers.

3. Combine butter, salt, ginger, cinnamon, and honey; fill each cavity with mixture. Return to oven; bake 2 minutes; turn plate halfway, and bake 2 minutes longer.

Makes 2 servings.

Butternut Squash Elegante

1 butternut squash (about 1
pound)
1 tablespoon butter
¾ teaspoon salt
⅛ teaspoon pepper
Elegant Parsley Sauce
(page 32)

1. Scrub squash. Make 2 slits on sides of the neck of the squash with knife. Make 2 more slits in body of squash. Stand squash on paper plate. Cook in microwave oven 8 minutes. Let stand 5 minutes.

2. Cut squash in half lengthwise. Discard seeds. Scoop squash out of shell. Combine with butter, salt, and pepper; beat lightly.

3. Serve with Elegant Parsley Sauce.

Makes 2 servings.

Herbed Summer Squash

3 yellow summer squash (about
1 pound)
2 tablespoons beef bouillon
1½ tablespoons butter
½ teaspoon salt
¾ teaspoon rosemary
¾ teaspoon oregano

1. Scrub squash; cut stem ends. Cut crosswise into ½-inch slices. Place in 1½-quart glass casserole. Add beef bouillon. Cook, covered, in microwave oven 6 to 6½ minutes or until tender. Drain well.

2. Add butter, salt, rosemary, and oregano; lightly toss with squash slices.

Makes 4 servings.

Honolulu Yams

1. Pare yams; slice ½ inch thick. Place in 2-quart glass casserole. Sprinkle with salt.

2. Add water. Cook, covered, in microwave oven 15 minutes, stirring once, after 10 minutes cooking time. Drain.

3. Arrange ½ of yam slices in 1½-quart glass casserole. Spoon ½ of pineapple; sprinkle with 2 tablespoons brown sugar. Dot with 1 tablespoon butter. Repeat layers.

4. Combine remaining sugar and butter with cinnamon; spread over top. Bake, uncovered, 4 minutes.

5. Let stand 5 minutes before serving.

Makes 4 servings.

2 pounds yams (about 4 yams)
¼ teaspoon salt
¼ cup water
1 can crushed pineapple
  (1 pound)
⅔ cup brown sugar
2½ tablespoons butter
dash cinnamon

Old-Fashioned Zucchini Custard

1. Place zucchini in bowl; sprinkle salt and let stand 1 hour. Turn into colander; press out all liquid.

2. Combine zucchini, cheese, pepper, garlic powder, parsley, celery, and biscuit mix. Stir in beaten eggs; stir until thoroughly mixed.

3. Place butter in 9-inch square glass baking dish. Heat in microwave oven 30 seconds until melted. Spread over bottom and sides of dish.

4. Pour zucchini mixture into baking dish. Cook, uncovered, 10 minutes, stirring once.

5. Let stand 5 minutes before serving. Garnish with olive halves.

Makes 6 servings.

5 cups shredded zucchini
1 teaspoon salt
1 cup shredded Swiss cheese
⅛ teaspoon pepper
⅛ teaspoon garlic powder
2 tablespoons chopped parsley
2 tablespoons chopped celery
¼ cup biscuit mix
4 well-beaten eggs
1 tablespoon butter
3 stuffed green olives, halved

119

Zucchini Bolognese

1 pound small, fresh
zucchini
2 stalks celery
1 can tomato sauce (8 ounces)
⅛ teaspoon garlic powder
½ teaspoon salt
⅛ teaspoon pepper
⅛ teaspoon oregano
⅛ teaspoon basil
⅛ teaspoon rosemary
2 tablespoons olive oil
2 tablespoons grated Parmesan
cheese

1. Scrub zucchini; slice ¼ inch thick. Slice celery ⅛ inch thick. Place in 1½-quart glass casserole.

2. Combine tomato sauce, garlic powder, salt, pepper, oregano, basil, rosemary, and oil; mix thoroughly. Pour over zucchini.

3. Sprinkle with cheese. Cook, covered, in microwave oven 7 minutes. Stir. Cook 6 to 7 minutes longer or until zucchini is just tender.

4. Let stand 5 minutes before serving.

Makes 4 servings.

Cereals and Pastas

Cooking cereal in the microwave oven is very easy and convenient. For individual servings, measure the amounts of ingredients right into the serving bowl or dish. As cereals tend to boil over quickly, use a larger bowl than usual, or if you are preparing a large quantity of cereal, use a large glass cooking utensil.

This being a split-second cooking operation, we suggest that the cereals be watched carefully.

After cooking, let the cereal stand, covered, 3 minutes before serving.

Macaroni, spaghetti, noodles, and rice may be cooked in the microwave oven very easily, but limit the quantity to 4 servings. For a larger quantity, cook the amount twice.

Individual Serving of Oatmeal

¼ cup quick-cooking
oatmeal
½ cup water
⅛ teaspoon salt

1. Measure oatmeal into large serving or soup bowl. Add water and salt; stir.

2. Cook, uncovered, in microwave oven 1 minute and 15 seconds. Stir; cover and let stand 3 minutes before serving.

Makes 1 serving.

Quantity Oatmeal

1½ cups quick-cooking
oatmeal
3 cups water
¾ teaspoon salt

1. Measure oatmeal into 2-quart glass casserole. Add water and salt; stir well.

2. Cook, uncovered, in microwave oven 4 minutes. Stir. Cook 2 minutes longer. Stir well.

3. Let stand, covered, 4 minutes before serving.

Makes 4 to 6 servings.

Kentucky Cornmeal Mush

1 cup yellow cornmeal
4 cups water
1½ teaspoons salt

1. Measure cornmeal into 3-quart glass casserole. Add water and salt; stir well.

2. Cook, uncovered, 5 minutes. Stir. Cook 5 minutes longer. Stir well.

3. Let stand, covered, 5 minutes before serving.

Makes 4 to 6 servings.

Regular Oatmeal

1½ cups regular oatmeal
3 cups water
¾ teaspoon salt

1. Measure oatmeal into 2-quart glass casserole. Add water and salt. Stir well.

2. Cook, uncovered, in microwave oven 8 minutes, stirring once. When cooking is completed, stir well.

3. Let stand, covered, 4 minutes before serving.

Makes 4 to 6 servings.

Dumplings

1. Combine flour, salt, and baking powder. Cut in shortening.

2. Stir in milk, just until dry ingredients are moistened.

3. Pour stock in 2-quart glass casserole. Heat to boiling, about 10 to 14 minutes, in microwave oven.

4. Drop the dough by rounded teaspoonfuls on top of the boiling stock. Cook, uncovered, 5 minutes.

5. Remove from oven. Let stand, covered, 5 minutes. Serve at once.

Makes 4 servings.

1 cup flour
½ teaspoon salt
1½ teaspoons baking powder
2 tablespoons shortening
⅔ cup milk
2½ cups chicken or beef stock

How to Cook Rice

Use regular rice, long grain or white-and-wild rice. Precooked rice requires only the addition of boiling water, or cooking to boiling point and allowing to stand, covered, for several minutes. Follow package directions and cook about ¼ the time required for surface cooking.

Regular Rice

1. Pour water in 2-quart glass casserole. Bring to boil in microwave oven, 8 to 10 minutes.

2. Add rice and salt; stir well. Cook, covered, 7 minutes.

3. Let stand, covered, 10 minutes. Fluff rice with fork before serving.

Makes 6 servings.

2½ cups water
1 cup regular rice
1 teaspoon salt

How to
Cook Pastas

Use macaroni, spaghetti, noodles, and other pastas. For wide pastas, such as lasagne, place pasta in 9 x 5 x 3-inch glass loaf pan.

Any Pasta

2 cups any pasta
3 teaspoons salt
6 cups boiling water

1. Place pasta in 2½-quart glass casserole. Add salt and boiling water; stir.

2. Cook, uncovered, in microwave oven 6 minutes. Stir.

3. Let stand, covered, 10 minutes. Drain thoroughly before serving.

Makes 4 servings.

Louisiana Rice

1 cup long-grain rice
1 tablespoon butter
1 pound ground lean beef
2 cups chopped celery
1 cup chopped green pepper
1 cup chopped onion
½ teaspoon salt
1 tablespoon garlic salt
½ teaspoon cumin powder
½ teaspoon thyme
2 tablespoons chili powder
1 cup sour cream
3 tomatoes, cut in wedges

1. Cook rice according to directions on page 123.

2. Place butter in 2-quart glass casserole; heat in microwave oven 30 seconds until melted.

3. Add beef; cook 5 minutes, stirring occasionally to break up meat.

4. Add celery, green pepper, and onion. Cook, covered, 7 minutes, stirring 3 times during cooking.

5. Combine salt, garlic salt, cumin, thyme, chili powder, and sour cream; blend well. Add to meat mixture along with rice; mix thoroughly.

6. Place tomato wedges on top of casserole mixture. Cook, covered, 5 minutes. Stir. Cook, uncovered, 3 minutes longer.

7. Let stand 10 minutes before serving.

Makes 6 to 8 servings.

Spaghetti al Dente

1. Cook spaghetti in microwave oven according to directions on page 124.

2. Combine beef, onion, and green pepper in 2½-quart casserole. Cook, covered, stirring occasionally for 10 minutes.

3. Add tomato soup, water, salt, and pepper; cook, uncovered, 1 minute.

4. Stir in cheese cubes. Cook, covered, 9 minutes, stirring once.

5. Let stand 5 minutes before serving.

Makes 4 servings.

2 cups spaghetti
1½ pounds ground lean beef
¼ cup chopped onion
¼ cup chopped green pepper
1 can tomato soup (10½ ounces)
¾ soup can water
1 teaspoon salt
⅛ teaspoon pepper
½ pound process American cheese, cubed

Macaroni and Cheese Chelsea

1. Cook macaroni in microwave oven according to directions on page 124.

2. Place butter in glass bowl; heat 30 seconds until melted.

3. Stir in flour; blend to a smooth paste.

4. Gradually add milk, stirring constantly until smooth. Cook 3 minutes.

5. Add salt and Worcestershire sauce; cook 1 minute longer. Stir in cheese until melted.

6. Place cooked macaroni in 2-quart glass casserole. Pour sauce over macaroni. Cook, covered, 6 minutes.

7. Top with tomato slices. Cook, uncovered, 3 minutes longer.

Makes 6 servings.

2 cups elbow macaroni
2 tablespoons butter
2 tablespoons flour
2 cups milk
1 teaspoon salt
1 teaspoon Worcestershire sauce
2 cups shredded sharp Cheddar cheese
6 tomato slices

Noodles Neapolitan

1 pound ground lean beef
1 tablespoon margarine
1 ½ cups uncooked noodles
1 teaspoon minced onion
1 ½ cups tomato juice
1 teaspoon salt
½ teaspoon pepper
¼ teaspoon oregano
1 tablespoon tomato paste
1 can peas (16 ounces),
drained

1. Place beef and margarine in 2-quart glass casserole; cook in microwave oven 2 minutes, stirring occasionally.

2. Sprinkle uncooked noodles and minced onion over the meat. Pour tomato juice over all. Cook, covered, 15 minutes, stirring once.

3. Add salt, pepper, oregano, and tomato paste; blend well. Add peas; stir. Cook, uncovered, 3 minutes.

4. Let stand, covered, 5 minutes before serving.

Makes 6 servings.

Egg and Cheese Dishes

The egg is an unpredictable product to cook in the shell in a microwave oven. The shell is porous and, as the egg ages, the air keeps penetrating the shell increasingly. Rapid heat, as applied by microwave, expands the gas (air) inside the shell with the result that the egg explodes.

It is possible, of course, to boil eggs by microwave by piercing the shells with a needle before placing them in the water, and then allowing them to stand in hot water for several minutes. But so little time is saved that this method is impractical.

Poached and scrambled eggs, and even omelettes, fare much better and are easier for a beginner to handle.

For even cooking, be sure poached eggs are completely covered with water. When cooking poached or fried eggs, be sure to puncture the yolk twice with the tines of a fork. This will break the surface membrane but the yolk will keep its shape.

The exact time for cooking eggs in a microwave oven will vary according to the

size and temperature, as well as the number of eggs prepared at one time. Always remember that cooked eggs, after they have been removed from the microwave oven, continue to cook and for this reason they should be removed while still underdone.

When preparing scrambled eggs, you must remember to stir the egg mixture frequently for a fluffier texture.

To fry eggs you must always place a glass of water in the microwave oven alongside of the plate with the egg. The glass of water will absorb some of the microwaves allowing the white and yolk to cook at the same rate of speed. Bacon cooked along with the egg helps retard overcooking of the yolk.

Baked Eggs

2 eggs
2 tablespoons light cream
1 teaspoon butter

1. Break 1 egg into each of 2 glass custard cups. With fork, carefully pierce yolk twice to break membrane. Spoon 1 tablespoon cream over each egg; dot with ½ teaspoon butter each. Cook in microwave oven 45 seconds, or to desired doneness.

Poached Eggs

2 eggs
2 cups boiling water
½ teaspoon salt

1. Pour boiling water into a 1-quart glass casserole. Break 1 egg at a time into a cup. With fork carefully pierce yolk twice to break membrane. Slide egg into hot water.

2. Cook 1 minute or to desired doneness. Drain well. Season with salt.

Scrambled Eggs

4 eggs
¼ cup light cream
¼ teaspoon salt
2 tablespoons butter

1. Combine eggs, cream and salt; beat with fork until well blended.

2. Place butter in glass pie plate; heat in microwave oven 30 seconds until melted.

3. Pour beaten eggs. Cook 1 minute. Stir. Cook 1½ minutes longer, stirring every 30 seconds. Remove from oven while eggs are still slightly softer than desired doneness.

128

Eggs Foo Yong

1. Combine cornstarch, sugar, and soy sauce in glass bowl; stir until blended.

2. Stir in water; heat in microwave oven 4 minutes, to simmering. Stir until smooth; set aside.

3. Beat eggs; add drained bean sprouts, onion, salt, pepper, and crab meat and blend well.

4. Pour ½ teaspoon vegetable oil in 5-inch shallow glass dish; heat 20 seconds.

5. Spoon 3 tablespoons of egg mixture onto glass dish; smooth out, like a pancake. Heat in oven 35 seconds. Continue until ingredients are used up. Stack egg pancakes in glass dish. Heat 1 minute.

6. If desired, roll up egg pancakes; spoon sauce over each serving and heat 20 seconds.

Makes 6 servings.

1 tablespoon cornstarch
1 tablespoon sugar
3 tablespoons soy sauce
1½ cups water
6 eggs
1 can bean sprouts (10½ ounces), drained
2 tablespoons instant minced onion
¾ teaspoon salt
¼ teaspoon pepper
1 cup canned crab meat, flaked
vegetable oil

Eggs Polonaise

1. Poach eggs in microwave oven according to directions on page 128; drain well and keep warm.

2. Place butter in glass baking dish; heat 1 minute until melted.

3. Add beef; heat 2 to 3 minutes, stirring twice, until it has lost its pink color.

4. Add tomato sauce, salt, and pepper; stir to blend well. Heat 4 minutes.

5. Arrange poached eggs on top; surround with toast points and sprinkle with parsley. Serve at once.

Makes 4 servings.

4 eggs
1 tablespoon butter
¾ pound ground lean beef
1 can tomato sauce (8 ounces)
¾ teaspoon salt
⅛ teaspoon pepper
4 slices bread, toasted, cut in half diagonally
2 tablespoons chopped parsley

Zesty Eggs with Cheeese

⅓ cup mayonnaise
¼ teaspoon salt
⅛ teaspoon pepper
½ teaspoon paprika
½ teaspoon Worcestershire
sauce
½ cup milk
1 cup grated sharp Cheddar
cheese
8 eggs

1. Combine mayonnaise, salt, pepper, paprika, and Worcestershire sauce in glass bowl; stir in milk until blended and smooth. Heat in microwave oven 1 minute.

2. Add cheese; stir. Cook in oven 3 minutes, stirring once.

3. Spoon 2 tablespoons of sauce into each of 4 individual glass baking dishes or custard cups.

4. Break 2 eggs into each dish; with fork carefully pierce yolk twice to break membrane. Spoon remaining sauce over the top.

5. Bake 5 to 7 minutes, turning dishes every minute until eggs are set to desired doneness.

6. Place each dish on serving plate and serve.

Makes 4 servings.

Eggs Andalouse

1. In glass bowl combine tomatoes, onion, bay leaf, cloves, sugar, and salt; heat in microwave oven 5 minutes. Strain; set aside.

2. Place butter in glass bowl; heat 1 minute until melted.

3. Stir in flour; heat 25 seconds.

4. Add strained tomato mixture; heat 4 minutes until thickened. Stir to smoothness.

5. Grease a shallow 2½-quart glass baking dish; spread rice evenly in bottom.

6. Make 4 hollows in rice with back of spoon. Break an egg into each hollow. Pierce yolk with fork.

7. Spoon sauce over all; sprinkle with cheese and bread crumbs.

8. Cover with plastic film, make puncture in center to allow steam to escape. Heat in oven 1 to 3 minutes until eggs are set to desired doneness. Serve by lifting each section of rice and egg with wide spatula onto plate.

Makes 4 servings.

1½ cups canned tomatoes
1½ tablespoons coarsely chopped onion
½ small bay leaf
2 cloves
¾ teaspoon sugar
½ teaspoon salt
1½ tablespoons butter
1½ tablespoons flour
2¼ cups cooked rice
4 eggs
2½ tablespoons grated Cheddar cheese
5 tablespoons buttered bread crumbs

Eggs in a Basket

1. Halve shredded wheat biscuits lengthwise; place on individual serving plates, two halves forming a nest.

2. Pour milk into bowl, heat in microwave oven to scalding, about 3 to 4 minutes. Add butter; stir, until melted.

3. Break eggs into milk and poach to desired doneness, according to directions on page 128. Remove bowl from oven.

4. Place 2 plates at a time in oven and heat shredded wheat biscuits 25 seconds.

5. Spoon egg-and-milk mixture over top of warmed shredded wheat biscuits. Season with salt and pepper; serve at once.

Makes 4 servings.

4 large shredded wheat biscuits
1½ cups milk
1½ tablespoons butter
4 eggs
½ teaspoon salt
⅛ teaspoon pepper

131

Western Poached Eggs

2 teaspoons butter
2 tablespoons chopped onion
1 can corned beef hash
(1 pound)
4 eggs
½ teaspoon salt
⅛ teaspoon pepper
chili sauce

1. Place butter in flat shallow baking dish; heat in microwave oven 50 seconds until melted.

2. Add onion; heat 75 seconds, stirring once.

3. Add corned beef hash; break it up with spoon. Heat 2 minutes, stirring twice.

4. Pat hash level in pan; make 4 deep hollows with back of spoon. Break an egg in each hollow; season with salt and pepper. Pierce yolk.

5. Cover pan with plastic film; slash center to allow heat to escape.

6. Heat in oven 1 to 3 minutes until eggs are set to desired doneness. Divide into 4 portions. With wide spatula carefully lift out each portion and place on serving plate. Serve with chili sauce.

Makes 4 servings.

Eggs Benedict

4 eggs
2 hamburger buns, split,
toasted
4 thin, small, cooked ham
slices
Hollandaise Sauce (page 34)
paprika

1. Poach eggs in microwave oven according to directions on page 128. Drain well; keep warm.

2. Place hamburger halves on shallow baking dish; arrange ham slices on top. Top with poached eggs.

3. Pour Hollandaise Sauce over all. Heat in microwave oven 1 minute.

4. Sprinkle with paprika; serve at once.

Makes 4 servings.

Egg and Tuna Coneys

1. Drain tuna fish; flake with fork until completely separated.

2. Combine eggs, green pepper, and onion; moisten with ½ the mayonnaise.

3. Combine olives, pickles and cheese; moisten with ½ the mayonnaise; heat in microwave oven 50 seconds.

4. Add egg mixture to olive mixture; blend well.

5. Fill frankfurter buns with mixture; place in covered glass pan, or wrap each bun completely with plastic film. Heat in oven as follows: 6 minutes for buns placed in covered glass pan, or 35 seconds for each bun.

Makes 8 to 10 servings.

1 can tuna fish (3½ ounces)
3 hard-cooked eggs, chopped
2 tablespoons chopped green pepper
2 tablespoons chopped onion
½ cup mayonnaise
2 tablespoons chopped green stuffed olives
2 tablespoons chopped sweet pickles
1 cup diced Cheddar cheese
8 to 10 frankfurter buns

Amsterdam Eggs and Ham

1. Place butter in glass baking dish; heat in microwave oven 1 minute.

2. Add onion; heat 25 seconds.

3. Stir in flour, salt, mustard, pepper, and Worcestershire sauce; heat 1 minute, stirring once.

4. Add milk; heat 5 minutes, stirring twice, until thickened.

5. Sprinkle ½ of cracker crumbs in bottom of buttered 2-quart casserole. Top with layers of sliced egg, ham, and sauce, ending with eggs. Sprinkle with remaining crumbs. Heat 5 to 6 minutes, or until sauce bubbles.

Makes 4 to 6 servings.

3 tablespoons butter
2 tablespoons minced onion
¼ cup flour
1 teaspoon salt
1 teaspoon dry mustard
⅛ teaspoon pepper
2 teaspoons Worcestershire sauce
2 cups milk
1 cup cracker crumbs
6 hard-cooked eggs, sliced
2 cups cubed cooked ham

Eggs Florentine

1 package frozen chopped
spinach (12 ounces)
½ teaspoon salt
1 tablespoon butter
4 poached eggs (page 128)
1¼ cups Mornay Sauce
(page 36)

1. Place frozen spinach in glass dish; sprinkle with salt. Do not add water. Heat in microwave oven 6 minutes, separating unthawed portion after 3 minutes. Drain well.

2. Line individual ramekins with spinach mixed with butter.

3. Arrange 1 poached egg on top of spinach in each ramekin. Cover with Mornay Sauce. Heat in oven, 2 ramekins at a time, 2 minutes or until sauce is bubbly.

Makes 4 servings.

Pink Cheese Rarebit

1 can tomato soup
(10½ ounces)
1 pound Cheddar cheese,
grated
2 eggs, separated
½ teaspoon paprika
1 teaspoon brown sugar
dash cayenne
4 slices white bread,
toasted

1. Pour tomato soup into 2-quart glass casserole. Stir in cheese. Cook, covered, in microwave oven 2 minutes. Stir. Cook 1½ minutes longer.

2. Beat egg yolks with paprika, sugar, and cayenne; stir into cheese mixture. Cook 1 minute.

3. Whip egg whites until stiff; fold into tomato mixture. Blend well. Serve over toast.

Makes 4 servings.

Lausanne Cheese Fondue

4 slices white bread, day
old preferred
1 tablespoon soft butter
½ pound shredded Swiss
cheese
2 eggs
½ cup milk
½ cup light cream
½ teaspoon salt
¼ teaspoon paprika
1/8 teaspoon cayenne
½ teaspoon dry mustard

1. Spread bread slices on one side with butter. Place in 8-inch square glass baking pan, buttered side up.

2. Sprinkle cheese over top.

3. Beat eggs lightly; add milk, cream, salt, paprika, and cayenne, and beat until blended. Pour egg mixture over cheese.

4. Cook in microwave oven 8 minutes or until just set, rotating pan every 2 minutes.

5. Let stand 5 minutes before serving.

Makes 4 servings.

Soups

Soups are satisfying fare for everyone because there is a soup for every taste. For emergency meals, canned soups may be heated right in the bowl in the microwave oven in minutes and they are ready to serve.

Homemade soup cooked in the microwave oven has a distinct fresh-made flavor that really can't be matched. When making soup from scratch, remember to use a large glass utensil to prevent boil-over, especially in the case of cream soups and chowders which contain milk.

To heat canned soup, place contents in a 1½-quart glass casserole; stir in 1 soup can of water. Heat, covered, 6 to 8 minutes or until soup bubbles. Stir and serve.

Hearty Beef-and-Vegetable Soup

1 pound ground lean beef
½ cup chopped onion
3 cups beef bouillon
5 cups water
2½ teaspoons salt
¼ teaspoon pepper
1 tablespoon chopped parsley
1 cup medium noodles
1 cup cut-up pared potatoes
1 cup shredded cabbage
½ cup cut-up, pared, carrots
½ cup chopped celery
½ cup frozen peas
2 cups canned tomatoes

1. Place beef in 4-quart glass casserole; separate with fork. Add onion. Cook, covered, in microwave oven 5 minutes. Stir; cook 5 minutes longer.

2. Combine bouillon and water; stir into beef mixture. Add salt, pepper, and parsley. Cook 10 minutes.

3. Add noodles, potatoes, cabbage, carrots, celery, peas, and tomatoes; cook 25 minutes until vegetables are tender, stirring once.

4. Let stand 10 minutes before serving.

5. If desired, refrigerate until needed. To serve, spoon into individual soup bowls. Heat in microwave oven 4 minutes.

Makes 10 servings.

Manhattan Clam Chowder

3 bacon slices, diced
¼ cup finely chopped onion
¼ cup finely chopped celery
¼ cup finely chopped carrots
1 medium potato, pared, diced
3 tablespoons flour
1 can minced clams
(7½ ounces)
1 cup clam juice
2 cups canned tomatoes
½ teaspoon thyme
1 bay leaf
¾ teaspoon salt
¼ teaspoon pepper

1. Place diced bacon in 3-quart glass casserole. Cook, uncovered, in microwave oven 2 minutes.

2. Add onion, celery, carrots, and potato, cook 2 minutes, stirring once.

3. Blend in flour until smooth. Add clams, clam juice, and tomatoes; cook 5 minutes.

4. Add thyme, bay leaf, salt, and pepper; cook 12 minutes longer.

5. Let stand 5 minutes before serving.

6. Remove bay leaf.

Makes 6 servings.

Old-Fashioned Split Pea Soup

1. Place peas in 3½-quart glass casserole; pour water into casserole, stir. Cook in microwave oven 10 minutes. Stir.

2. Add ham bone, onion, carrot, potato, parsley sprigs, salt, pepper, thyme, and chicken broth; stir until blended. Cook 5 minutes.

3. Add ham; cook 20 minutes longer, stirring every 10 minutes.

4. Let soup stand 5 minutes before serving.

5. Remove ham bone and discard.

Makes 8 servings.

1½ pounds dry green split peas
1 quart water
1 ham bone
⅔ cup coarsely chopped onion
¼ cup cut-up carrot
1 small potato, pared, cubed
2 parsley sprigs
¼ teaspoon salt
⅛ teaspoon pepper
⅛ teaspoon thyme
3½ cups chicken broth
1 pound smoked ham, cubed

Early American Corn Soup

1. Pour water in 2½-quart glass casserole. Heat in microwave oven 4 to 5 minutes to boiling point.

2. Stir in bouillon cubes until dissolved.

3. Add corn, salt, pepper, and onion; stir until blended.

4. Combine flour with 2 tablespoons cream; blend to a smooth paste. Gradually stir in cream and egg yolks, stirring constantly, until smooth.

5. Add cream mixture to corn mixture; cook, uncovered, 5 minutes until bubbly, stirring twice during cooking time.

6. Let stand, covered, 5 minutes before serving.

Makes 4 servings.

2 cups water
3 chicken bouillon cubes
1 cup cooked corn
½ teaspoon salt
⅛ teaspoon pepper
1 teaspoon minced onion
2 tablespoons flour
1 cup light cream
2 slightly beaten egg yolks

French Onion Soup

¼ cup butter
4 cups thinly sliced onions
4 cans beef bouillon (10½
ounces each)
1 teaspoon salt
6 slices French bread, 1 inch
thick, toasted
3 tablespoons grated Parmesan
cheese

1. Place butter in 3½-quart glass casserole; heat in microwave oven 1 minute until melted.

2. Add onions; cook 3 minutes, stirring once.

3. Add bouillon and salt. Cook, covered, 20 minutes, stirring after each 5 minutes.

4. Let stand, covered, 5 minutes.

5. To serve, ladle soup into 6 individual soup bowls; add slice of French bread, sprinkle with Parmesan cheese.

6. Place 2 bowls at a time in microwave oven, heat 30 seconds.

Makes 6 servings.

Vichyssoise Chantillon

1 medium onion, minced
3 minced leeks, white part
only
2 tablespoons butter
2 cups finely diced potatoes
4 cups chicken broth
1 cup heavy cream
½ teaspoon salt
⅛ teaspoon pepper
1 tablespoon chopped chives

1. Place onion, leeks, and butter in 2½-quart glass casserole; cook 2 minutes, stirring once.

2. Add potatoes and chicken broth, Cook, covered, 15 to 16 minutes or until potatoes are very tender.

3. Press potato mixture through fine sieve; return to casserole.

4. Add cream, salt, and pepper; heat 3 minutes until soup is hot but not boiling.

5. Let stand, uncovered, to cool. Chill thoroughly in refrigerator.

6. Serve sprinkled with chives.

Makes 4 servings.

Moscow Borscht

1. Place butter and onion in 2½-quart glass casserole. Cook, uncovered, in microwave oven 2½ minutes.

2. Press onion and beets through fine sieve; return to casserole.

3. Add consommé, salt, Tabasco; cook 5 minutes until soup is hot but not boiling.

4. Stir in lemon juice.

5. Let stand 5 minutes before serving.

6. To serve: spoon soup into 4 individual bowls; garnish with sour cream and sprinkle with chives.

Makes 4 servings.

2 tablespoons butter
½ cup minced onion
1 can diced beets (1 pound)
2 cups consommé
½ teaspoon salt
3 dashes Tabasco
1 tablespoon lemon juice
¼ cup sour cream
1 teaspoon chopped chives

Polish Lentil Soup

1. Wash lentils; drain. Place in 3½-quart glass casserole. Add 2 cups water. Cook, covered, in microwave oven 2 minutes. Remove from oven; let stand, covered, 1½ hours.

2. Add remaining 2 cups water to lentils, carrot, potato, onion, celery, and parsley. Cook, covered, 14 minutes. Stir thoroughly.

3. Slice sausage; add to soup with salt. Cook 15 to 20 minutes longer until vegetables are tender.

4. Place butter in bowl; melt 1 minute. Stir in flour to make smooth paste. Stir into soup. Heat 2 minutes.

Makes 6 servings.

½ cup dry lentils
4 cups water
1 small carrot, diced
1 small potato, diced
¼ cup minced onion
2 tablespoons minced celery
2 tablespoons minced parsley
½ pound Polish sausage
1 teaspoon salt
1 tablespoon butter
1 tablespoon flour

New Orleans Gumbo

½ pound ground veal
¼ cup minced onion
4 cups water
2 cups fresh okra, cut in
1-inch pieces
1 can tomatoes (10 ounces)
½ cup finely chopped green
pepper
¼ teaspoon thyme
1 teaspoon salt
⅛ teaspoon pepper
½ teaspoon basil
2 tablespoons flour
2 tablespoons butter

1. Place veal and onion in 3½-quart glass casserole. Cook, covered, in microwave oven 5 minutes. Stir; cook 5 minutes longer.

2. Add water, okra, tomatoes, green pepper, thyme, salt, pepper, and basil. Cook 20 to 25 minutes or until okra is tender, stirring twice during cooking time.

3. Combine flour and butter; blend to a smooth paste. Stir into soup until well blended. Cook 3 minutes.

4. Let stand, covered, 5 minutes before serving.

Makes 6 to 8 servings.

Boston Oyster Chowder

¼ cup butter
½ pint oysters with liquid
1 cup milk
½ cup light cream
½ cup heavy cream
½ teaspoon salt
⅛ teaspoon white pepper
½ teaspoon Worcestershire
sauce
2 drops Tabasco
1 tablespoon chopped parsley

1. Place butter in 2-quart glass casserole. Add oysters; cook, uncovered, in microwave oven, 1 minute.

2. Combine oyster liquid, milk, light and heavy cream; blend well. Pour over oysters.

3. Add salt, pepper, Worcestershire sauce, and Tabasco. Cook 3 to 3½ minutes longer, just until milk begins to bubble. Do not allow to boil.

4. Cover casserole; let stand 3 minutes before serving.

5. Sprinkle parsley just before serving.

Makes 4 servings.

Appetizers, Snacks and Beverages

The microwave oven is the invisible chef when entertaining, from casual drop-ins to formal parties, for after-the-school snacks, and for impromptu kaffee-klatsches.

After serving your pièce de résistance, don't be surprised if your microwave oven becomes the conversation piece.

Appetizers may be prepared early in the day and refrigerated until serving time. Remember to wrap them in waxed paper, plastic film, or freezer paper, then you can transfer them directly to the oven for heating. Avoid using aluminum foil since the microwaves will not penetrate and you may have difficulty unwrapping frozen items.

The club gang or the football team will never catch you unprepared. You can serve hot sandwiches in minutes along with appetizing beverages.

Continental Hors d'Oeuvre

*1 package soft cream cheese
(3 ounces)
¼ cup crumbled Roquefort
cheese
¼ cup finely chopped almonds
½ teaspoon Worcestershire
sauce
dash Tabasco
1 teaspoon crumbled bacon
crisp cocktail crackers*

1. Combine cream cheese, Roquefort cheese, almonds, Worcestershire sauce, Tabasco, and bacon; blend thoroughly.

2. Spread mixture on crackers, using about 1 heaping teaspoon for each cracker.

3. Arrange 12 crackers on absorbent paper laid out in a circle in microwave oven. Heat 45 to 55 seconds until cheese begins to bubble. Serve hot.

Makes 10 servings.

Rumaki

*½ pound chicken livers
1 can water chestnuts
(6 ounces), drained
5 slices bacon
soy sauce*

1. Cut chicken livers in half, or into thirds if they are large.

2. Cut water chestnuts in half.

3. Cut bacon slices in half.

4. Dip livers in soy sauce; brush each half-slice of bacon on one side with soy sauce.

5. Place 1 piece of liver and 1 slice of water chestnut on ½ slice of bacon; roll up and secure with wooden pick. Place on paper plate lined with a double layer of absorbent paper. Cover rumakis with 1 layer of absorbent paper. Heat in microwave oven 5 minutes. Serve hot.

Makes 10 servings.

Oriental Cocktail Kabobs

1. Combine soy sauce and Worcestershire sauce, sugar, vinegar, and ginger; blend well.

2. Cut ham into small ¼-inch cubes.

3. Cut pineapple chunks in two.

4. Using wooden picks, skewer 1 piece of ham, then 1 piece of pineapple. Top with

1 mushroom cap, resting on tip of wooden pick like a crown.

5. Place 18 kabobs in a circle on paper plate covered with absorbent paper; cook 1½ minutes. Turn kabobs; spoon soy mixture over them, brushing to coat evenly. Cook 2 minutes longer.

6. Repeat with remaining kabobs and soy mixture. Serve hot.

Makes 36 appetizers.

1½ tablespoons soy sauce
½ teaspoon Worcestershire sauce
1 tablespoon brown sugar
1 tablespoon wine vinegar
dash powdered ginger
36 small cubes of cooked ham
18 canned pineapple chunks
36 tiny canned mushroom caps

Cantonese Meatballs

1. Shape beef into tiny meatballs, about ¼-inch in size. Place in shallow glass baking pan.

2. Add onion, salt, tomato sauce, lemon juice, sugar, and Tabasco; stir well to blend. Cook in microwave oven, uncovered, stirring twice.

3. Add pineapple chunks. Heat 1 minute longer. Serve hot with wooden picks as appetizers.

Makes 6 servings.

½ pound ground lean beef
1 small onion, finely chopped
½ teaspoon seasoned salt
½ cup canned tomato sauce
1½ tablespoons lemon juice
2 tablespoons brown sugar
dash Tabasco
½ cup pineapple chunks, halved, drained

Oriental Orange Dip

1. Combine lemon juice, water, soy sauce, and Worcestershire sauce in glass dish; stir until blended.

2. Add garlic and marmalade; stir well.

3. Heat in microwave oven 2 minutes or until very hot.

4. Serve hot as a dip for miniature pork meatballs, or tiny codfish cakes.

Makes about 1 cup.

2 tablespoons lemon juice
⅓ cup water
¼ cup soy sauce
dash Worcestershire sauce
1 clove garlic, minced
⅓ cup orange marmalade

Swiss Fondue au Kirsch

1 clove garlic, cut in half
1 pound Swiss cheese, grated
dash salt
dash pepper
dry white wine
¼ cup cornstarch
2 tablespoons water
2 tablespoons kirsch
1 loaf French bread, cut
into 1-inch cubes

1. Rub side and bottom of glass or crockery dish with garlic; discard garlic.

2. Combine cheese, salt, and pepper in dish; add enough wine to barely cover. Stir until well blended.

3. Heat in microwave oven 1 minute and 10 seconds, just until the cheese melts.

4. Combine cornstarch and water to make smooth paste; add kirsch and blend well. Stir mixture into wine mixture until smooth.

5. Heat in oven 1½ to 2 minutes or until fondue is creamy and thick.

6. Serve fondue in chafing dish over a flame or a substitute. Spear bread cubes with fork and dip in fondue.

Makes about 8 servings.

Smetana Mushrooms

1 pound large mushrooms
¼ pound ground lean beef
1 clove garlic, minced
3 tablespoons minced onion
1 tablespoon minced shallot
1 tablespoon minced parsley
½ teaspoon salt
1 teaspoon gravy coloring
2 tablespoons lemon juice
¼ cup sour cream

1. Choose mushrooms of uniform size. Wash them and carefully remove stems; chop stems finely.

2. Ask butcher to grind beef twice. Combine beef, chopped mushroom stems, garlic, onion, shallot, parsley, salt, gravy coloring, and ¼ teaspoon lemon juice in shallow glass baking dish; mix well. Cook in microwave oven 3 minutes, stirring mixture twice.

3. Dip each mushroom in remaining lemon juice; fill with beef mixture. Arrange 12 mushrooms at a time in a circle on glass pie plate. Bake in microwave oven 3½ to 4 minutes.

4. Serve piping hot with daub of sour cream.

Makes 8 servings.

Boston Nibbles

1. Combine bread crumbs, salt, paprika, and cayenne; mix thoroughly.

2. Cut bacon slices in half; then cut each piece in half again to form 4 strips for each bacon slice. Arrange half the strips on 2 layers of absorbent paper; cover the bacon with 2 layers of absorbent paper. Place remaining bacon strips on top; cover with 1 layer of absorbent paper. Cook in microwave oven 1½ to 2 minutes, just until bacon is limp.

3. Drain oysters on absorbent paper. Dip each oyster in cream, then roll in crumb mixture. Wrap 1 strip of bacon around oyster; fasten with wooden pick.

4. Arrange in a circle on paper plate covered with a double layer of absorbent paper, 10 at a time. Cook 2 minutes until bacon is crisp.

Makes 20 appetizers.

½ cup dry fine bread crumbs
¼ teaspoon salt
¼ teaspoon paprika
dash cayenne
5 slices bacon
20 canned smoked oysters,
  well drained
¼ cup light cream

Riverboat Shrimp Dainties

1. Shell shrimp leaving tails intact.

2. Place butter in glass bowl; heat in microwave oven 1 minute until melted.

3. Add chili powder, garlic powder, and Tabasco; stir until blended.

4. Cut bacon slices in half; then each piece into half again to form 4 strips for each slice.

5. Dip each shrimp into butter mixture, turning to coat evenly. Wrap a strip of bacon around shrimp; fasten with wooden pick. Place in a circle on paper plate covered with absorbent paper. Cook 3½ to 4 minutes until bacon is lightly browned.

6. Serve hot with lemon wedges.

Makes 12 appetizers.

12 medium-to-large fresh
  shrimp in shells
¼ cup butter
¾ teaspoon chili powder
dash garlic powder
dash Tabasco
3 slices bacon
6 lemon wedges

145

Mock Caviar Dip

1 large eggplant
¼ cup olive oil
6 tablespoons minced onion
2 tablespoons minced celery
¼ cup tomato paste
1 tablespoon lemon juice
½ teaspoon salt
¼ teaspoon pepper
½ teaspoon garlic powder

1. Place whole eggplant in shallow baking dish, cutting off stem only. Bake in microwave oven 10 to 12 minutes or until eggplant is soft. Let stand until cool.

2. Combine oil, onion, and celery in 1-quart glass casserole; cook 3 minutes, stirring once.

3. Peel eggplant; cut into sections and place in electric-blender container with onion mixture, tomato paste, lemon juice and ¼ teaspoon salt; blend 1 minute until smooth.

4. Season with remaining salt, pepper, and garlic powder.

5. To serve hot, heat in oven 1 minute; serve with corn chips or crisp crackers.

6. To serve cold, chill in refrigerator at least 2 hours; serve with chilled celery chunks.

Makes 8 to 10 servings.

Mexican Zip Dip

2 cans kidney beans (1 pound each)
¼ cup vegetable oil
1 cup grated Cheddar cheese
¼ teaspoon salt
¼ teaspoon onion salt
1½ teaspoons chili powder
¼ teaspoon paprika
corn chips

1. Drain beans; reserve liquid.

2. Combine beans, vegetable oil, and ⅓ cup bean liquid in glass or ceramic bowl; heat in microwave oven 4 minutes. Stir.

3. Remove from oven; mash and blend mixture until smooth.

4. Stir in cheese, salts, chili powder, and paprika; heat in oven 3 minutes or until cheese melts.

5. Remove from oven; stir. Serve hot with corn chips.

Makes about 2 cups.

146

South-of-the-Border Dip

1. In large 2½-quart glass casserole combine tomatoes, tomato paste, onions, garlic, and chile peppers; mix well. Cook in microwave oven 20 minutes, covered, stirring twice.

2. Add sugar and salt; stir. Cook 20 to 25 minutes longer, covered, until sauce is very thick.

3. Blend in cheese. Stir until melted.

4. Add cayenne; stir.

5. Let stand 5 minutes. Serve with toasted tortillas.

Makes 12 servings.

1 can tomatoes (1 pound, 13 ounces)
1 can tomato paste (6 ounces)
3 medium onions, finely chopped
1 large clove garlic, minced
4 canned green chili peppers, minced
1 teaspoon sugar
1 teaspoon salt
1½ cups grated sharp Cheddar cheese
dash cayenne

Sloppy Josés

1. Place beef in 1½-quart glass casserole; cook, covered, in microwave oven 5 minutes, stirring once to separate meat.

2. Add onion, tomato sauce, brown sugar, vinegar, mustard, chili powder, Worcestershire sauce, salt, and pepper; mix thoroughly.

3. Cook 2½ minutes, stirring once. Let stand 10 minutes to blend flavors.

4. Cook 2½ minutes longer, stirring once.

5. To serve, spoon hot mixture over split hamburger buns.

Makes 6 servings.

1 pound ground lean beef
1 small onion, chopped
½ cup canned tomato sauce
2 tablespoons brown sugar
2 tablespoons vinegar
2 teaspoons prepared mustard
¾ teaspoon chili powder
1 teaspoon Worcestershire sauce
¾ teaspoon salt
⅛ teaspoon pepper
6 hamburger buns

147

Rachel Sandwiches

4 slices toasted rye bread
2 thin slices cooked corned
beef
¼ cup sauerkraut, well
drained
2 slices Swiss cheese
2 teaspoons Thousand Island
dressing
½ teaspoon paprika

1. Place 1 slice of bread on each of 2 paper plates.

2. Cover with 1 slice each of corned beef. Spread with sauerkraut. Top with Swiss cheese.

3. Spread remaining 2 slices of bread with Thousand Island dressing; sprinkle with paprika. Place on top of cheese. Heat 1 sandwich at a time in microwave oven for 45 seconds until cheese has melted.

Makes 2 servings.

Western Sloppy Joes

1 pound ground lean beef
½ cup chopped onion
1 can tomato soup
(10½ ounces)
2 tablespoons chili sauce
1 teaspoon prepared mustard
½ teaspoon salt
¼ teaspoon pepper
6 hamburger buns, split,
toasted
6 tomato slices
6 onion slices
6 American cheese slices
paprika

1. Place meat in 2-quart glass casserole. Cook in microwave oven 5 minutes, stirring once.

2. Add onion, soup, chili sauce, mustard, salt, and pepper; mix thoroughly. Cook 5 minutes, stirring once.

3. Place 1 split hamburger bun on each of 6 serving plates; spoon in beef mixture. Top with 1 tomato slice, then 1 onion slice.

4. Place a slice of cheese on top of all; sprinkle with paprika placing 1 serving at a time in the oven, and heat 15 seconds or until cheese is slightly melted.

Makes 6 servings.

Early American Cocoa

1. Combine cocoa, cinnamon, nutmeg, and sugar in 1-quart glass casserole. Stir in

148

water; blend well. Heat in microwave oven, uncovered, 30 seconds.

2. Stir in milk; heat 5 to 5½ minutes until scalded but not boiling.

3. Serve hot with marshmallows on top.

Makes 2 servings.

6 tablespoons sweetened cocoa
⅛ teaspoon cinnamon
dash nutmeg
2 teaspoons sugar
½ cup boiling water
1 cup milk
2 marshmallows

Quick Hot Chocolate

1. Pour milk into ceramic mug; stir in chocolate and nutmeg until well blended. Heat 1½ minutes.

2. Serve immediately with daub of whipped cream.

Makes 1 serving.

¾ cup milk
1 tablespoon chocolate syrup
dash nutmeg
whipped cream

Austrian Mocha Chocolate

1. Combine chocolate, sugar, coffee, and salt in glass dish; heat in microwave oven 30 seconds, stirring to blend melted chocolate.

2. Stir in milk; blend well and heat, uncovered, 4 minutes.

3. Pour into 2 cups; serve topped with whipped cream.

Makes 2 servings.

1 square unsweetened chocolate (1 ounce)
1½ tablespoons sugar
1 cup leftover strong coffee
dash salt
1½ cups milk
whipped cream

Acapulco Chocolate

1. Pour milk into 2-quart glass casserole.

2. Add syrup, instant coffee, and mace; stir until well blended. Heat, covered, in microwave oven 8 to 10 minutes until milk is just scalded but not boiling.

3. Stir and pour into cups.

Makes 4 servings.

1 quart milk
¼ cup chocolate syrup
2 teaspoons instant coffee
dash mace

Swiss Hot Chocolate

3 milk chocolate bars
(1 ounce each)
½ cup water
3 cups milk
2 teaspoons instant coffee
⅛ teaspoon cinnamon
dash nutmeg
½ cup heavy cream, whipped
¼ teaspoon almond extract

1. Break chocolate bars into 2-quart glass casserole. Add water; heat in microwave oven 45 seconds.

2. Add milk, instant coffee, cinnamon, and nutmeg. Heat, uncovered, 7 to 8 minutes or until hot but not boiling.

3. Pour into mugs.

4. Combine whipped cream with almond extract. Top hot chocolate with spoonful.

Makes 4 servings.

Williamsburg Fruit Punch

12 whole cloves
4 lemon slices
1 cup apple cider
½ cup bottled cranberry juice
¼ cup orange juice
6 tablespoons canned apricot nectar
1 teaspoon lemon juice
4 sugar lumps
½ teaspoon cinnamon
⅛ teaspoon mace
dash nutmeg

1. Insert 3 cloves in each lemon slice; set aside.

2. Combine cider, cranberry juice, orange juice, apricot nectar, and lemon juice in deep glass bowl.

3. Add lemon slices; heat in microwave oven 12 minutes, or until hot. Pour into individual cups.

4. Toss sugar lumps with combined spices; add 1 sugar lump into each cup.

Makes 4 servings.

Party Spiced Punch

1 quart cranberry juice
1 quart unsweetened pineapple juice
1 stick cinnamon (3 inches)
¼ teaspoon allspice
6 whole cloves
dash mace
½ cup brown sugar

1. Combine cranberry and pineapple juice in 3-quart glass casserole.

2. Add cinnamon, allspice, cloves, mace, and sugar; stir until sugar is dissolved. Heat in microwave oven, covered, 13 to 14 minutes or until mixture is bubbly.

3. To serve, pour into ceramic mugs or pottery punch glasses; do not use plain glass unless punch is slightly cooled to avoid breaking the glass.

Makes about 2½ quarts.

Hot Tomato Aperitif

1. Combine tomato juice and consommé in 2-quart glass casserole. Heat in microwave oven 5 minutes, stirring once.

2. Add salt, pepper, Worcestershire sauce, cloves, bay leaf, onion, celery, and butter; mix thoroughly. Heat, covered, 10 minutes longer, stirring once.

3. Strain tomato mixture. Pour into ceramic mugs and serve hot.

Makes 8 servings.

4 cups tomato juice
1 cup consommé
½ teaspoon salt
¼ teaspoon pepper
¼ teaspoon Worcestershire sauce
3 whole cloves
1 bay leaf
1 tablespoon chopped onion
2 tablespoons chopped celery
1 tablespoon butter

Fruits

The microwave oven is ideal for the preparation of fruit dishes. Fruits retain their fresh fruit flavor and are so superior in taste that you would not wish to cook them any other way.

Always use caution in the cooking time and amount of sugar used when cooking fruits, as these may vary depending on ripeness of fruit and variety. Check at half-time for doneness. Be careful about tasting as the mixture will be very hot. Place spoon with small amount of mixture on an ice cube for a few seconds before tasting.

When cooking cut fruit, be sure that pieces are uniformly sized and well spaced in the baking utensil.

Jams and jellies may be prepared with ease in the microwave oven, but be sure that you use double the size of utensil volume as called for in the recipe yield to avoid spilling over. Times in preparation will be much shorter than in conventional cooking and these should be considered and frequently checked.

Do not attempt to melt paraffin in the microwave oven.

153

Cooking Chart for Fresh Fruits

Fruit	Amount	Cooking Instructions	Time in Minutes
Apples	4 medium (1½ pounds)	See special instructions in recipe, page 155.	
Apricots, dried	8 ounces	In 1 cup water, 3 tablespoons sugar; let stand in water 1 hour before adding sugar.	3½
Bananas	2 large	Quarter, space well in baking dish; brush with melted butter.	1½
Cranberries	1 pound	In 1 cup water, with 2 cups sugar; cook until cranberries pop.	8
Grapefruit	1, cut in half	In 2 teaspoons brown sugar, 1 teaspoon butter.	2½
Peaches fresh	8 medium	See special instructions in recipe, page 158.	
dried	8 ounces	In 1 cup water, with 3 tablespoons sugar; let stand in water 1 hour before adding sugar.	3½
Prunes, dried, tenderized	1 pound	In 1½ cups water, with dash cinnamon; let stand 30 minutes before cooking.	5
Rhubarb	2 cups	In 2 tablespoons water, ½ cup sugar, dash salt.	5

Baked Apples

1. Core apples; slice off a thin circle of peel, about ½ inch, from the top of each apple.

2. Arrange apples in a circle in a 9-inch glass cake pan. Spoon 1 tablespoon sugar into each cavity; top with ½ teaspoon butter. Cook, uncovered, in microwave oven, 4 to 5 minutes, or until apples are tender.

3. Let apples stand 3 minutes before serving.

Makes 4 servings.

4 apples (about 1½ pounds)
¼ cup sugar
2 teaspoons butter

Butterscotch Baked Apples

1. Wash and core apples; place on greased glass baking dish.

2. Combine ⅓ cup cream, ⅓ cup corn syrup, and walnuts; mix well. Fill centers of apples.

3. Heat in microwave oven 6 minutes until tender.

4. Combine remaining cream and corn syrup with butter and vanilla in glass bowl; heat in oven 4 minutes, stirring twice. Serve warm over apples.

Makes 4 servings.

4 baking apples
1⅓ cups light cream
⅔ cup dark corn syrup
⅓ cup chopped walnuts
2 tablespoons butter
1 teaspoon vanilla

155

Spicy Apple Betty

2 tablespoons butter
3 cups day-old bread cubes
3 tart apples, pared, sliced
½ cup brown sugar
¼ teaspoon cinnamon
⅛ teaspoon nutmeg
dash allspice
2 teaspoons lemon juice
2 tablespoons water
1 cup heavy cream, whipped

1. Place butter in glass bowl; heat in microwave oven 30 seconds until melted.

2. Add bread cubes; toss lightly until coated. Arrange ⅓ of buttered bread cubes in 9-inch glass square baking pan.

3. Combine apples, sugar, cinnamon, nutmeg, and allspice; mix well. Place ½ of apple mixture over bread cubes. Place ⅓ bread cubes on top of apples; arrange remaining apples, topped with remaining cubes. Combine lemon juice and water; sprinkle over the top.

4. If desired, dot with additional 2 tablespoons butter.

5. Cook, uncovered, 12 to 13 minutes or until apples are tender.

6. Let stand 3 minutes. Serve with whipped cream.

Makes 9 servings.

Apple Doodle

5 cups tart apples, pared, sliced
1 cup brown sugar
1 cup flour
¾ cup oatmeal
½ teaspoon salt
½ teaspoon cinnamon
¼ teaspoon nutmeg
¼ teaspoon powdered allspice
½ cup butter
Dorothy's Butterscotch Sauce (page 42)

1. Arrange apple slices evenly in a 12 x 9 x 2-inch glass baking dish.

2. Combine sugar, flour, oatmeal, salt, cinnamon, nutmeg, allspice, in bowl. Cut in butter with pastry blender until mixture is crumbly.

3. Sprinkle over sliced apples. Bake in microwave oven, uncovered, 15 minutes, turning pan at the end of each 5 minutes.

4. Let stand 10 minutes. Serve warm with Dorothy's Butterscotch Sauce.

Makes 8 servings.

Applesauce

4 cups tart apples, pared, sliced
½ cup water
⅓ cup sugar

1. Place apples in a 1½-quart glass casserole. Pour water over apples. Cook, covered, in microwave oven 6 to 7 minutes, or until apples are tender.

2. Press hot apples through fine sieve. Stir in sugar and blend well in hot mixture.

Makes about 4 cups.

Fresh Cranberry Sauce

1. Wash cranberries; drain, and remove stems. Place in 3-quart glass casserole.

2. Add sugar and water; stir well. Add orange peel; stir. Cook, covered, in microwave oven 8 to 10 minutes or until cranberries have popped and mixture has almost reached the top of the casserole. Let stand without stirring until cool.

3. Refrigerate overnight.

Makes 1 quart.

1 pound cranberries
3 cups sugar
2 cups water
1 tablespoon grated orange peel

Continental Grapefruit

1. Cut grapefruit in half; seed, if necessary. With sharp knife cut around each section.

2. Sprinkle sugar over top. Dot with butter; sprinkle with rum.

3. Place grapefruit halves on serving china dish. Bake, uncovered, in microwave oven 2½ minutes. Serve hot.

Makes 2 servings.

1 grapefruit
2 teaspoons brown sugar
1 teaspoon butter
1 teaspoon dark rum

Fresh Peach Delight

1. Peel peaches, cut in half and remove pits. Coat lightly with lemon juice.

2. Arrange peach halves in 9-inch square glass baking pan. Sprinkle tops with sugar. Fill centers with almonds. Sprinkle with nutmeg. Bake, uncovered, in microwave oven 5 to 7 minutes, turning pan twice during cooking.

3. Sprinkle brandy on top. Let stand 3 minutes.

Makes 4 servings.

4 peaches (about 2 pounds)
2 teaspoons lemon juice
2 tablespoons sugar
¼ cup chopped almonds
¼ teaspoon nutmeg
1½ teaspoons brandy

157

Baked Fresh Peaches

8 medium peaches
2 tablespoons lemon juice
¼ cup water
¾ cup flour
1 cup brown sugar
¼ teaspoon salt
⅛ teaspoon nutmeg
1 cup heavy cream, whipped

1. Peel peaches; slice. Place in 2-quart glass casserole.

2. Combine lemon juice and water; mix well. Pour over peaches.

3. Combine flour, sugar, salt, and nutmeg; mix well. Sprinkle over fruit. Bake, uncovered, in microwave oven 5 to 7 minutes, depending on ripeness of fruit.

4. Let stand 3 minutes. Serve warm with whipped cream.

Makes 4 servings.

Stewed Peaches with Vanilla Sauce

1 package dried peaches
(8 ounces)
1 cup water
3 tablespoons sugar
Quick Vanilla Sauce
(page 44)

1. Place peaches and water in 1½-quart glass casserole. Let stand 1 hour.

2. Add sugar; stir until blended. Cook, covered, in microwave oven 3½ minutes.

3. Let stand, covered, until warm. Serve with Quick Vanilla Sauce.

Makes 4 servings.

New England Baked Rhubarb

2 cups rhubarb, cleaned, cut
in ½-inch pieces
2 tablespoons water
dash salt
½ cup sugar
1 stick cinnamon (1 inch)
4 whole cloves

1. Place rhubarb and water in 2-quart glass casserole.

2. Add salt. Bake, covered, 4 minutes, stirring once.

3. Add sugar, cinnamon stick, and cloves; bake 1 minute longer.

4. Let stand, covered, until thoroughly cooled.

Makes 4 servings.

New York Rhubarb Crisp

1. Combine rhubarb, lemon juice, and sugar; mix well. Spread in bottom of 9-inch square glass baking dish.

2. Sprinkle lemon peel over the top.

3. Combine brown sugar, flour, rolled oats, and butter; mix together until crumbly. Sprinkle on top of rhubarb. Bake, uncovered, in microwave oven 15 minutes, turning pan 3 times.

4. Let stand 5 minutes. Serve with Custard Sauce Delong.

Makes 6 servings.

2 cups rhubarb, cleaned, cut in ½-inch pieces
2 tablespoons lemon juice
½ cup sugar
½ teaspoon grated lemon peel
1 cup brown sugar
¾ cup flour
¼ cup rolled oats
½ cup soft butter
Custard Sauce Delong
(page 42)

Desserts

The microwave oven is ideal for the preparation of many desserts ranging from custards and puddings to cakes and confections.

A few points should be taken into consideration for successful preparation.

Custards will continue to cook after they are removed from the oven, therefore caution should be exercised not to overcook them as overcooking will result in separation of the ingredients. Puddings and custards made with milk tend to boil over and frequent stirring is recommended.

Cakes do not brown, but since these are usually frosted it makes no difference.

Learn to use the microwave oven as a quick aid to making desserts.

To toast nuts: Spread about 1 cup walnuts, almonds, or other nuts on a paper plate in 1 layer and toast 2 to 3 minutes, stirring after the first minute.

To melt chocolate: Place a 1-ounce chocolate square in a dish and melt about 2 minutes, stirring twice. If recipe calls for soft chocolate for spreading, place the chocolate square in its wrapper, seam side up, in the oven; heat 1 minute to blending consistency.

To melt butter or margarine: To melt or soften butter or margarine use the same procedure as in melting chocolate, above.

To heat cake sauces and toppings: Pour 1 cup of sauce into a glass dish and warm for 30 seconds, if sauce is at room temperature, or 75 seconds if refrigerated.

To make gelatin desserts: Pour 1 cup of water in a 1-quart glass dish; heat 2 minutes. Remove from oven; add gelatin and stir until dissolved. Proceed with recipe.

Golden Custard

1¾ cups milk
3 eggs
¼ cup sugar
⅛ teaspoon salt
1 teaspoon vanilla
½ cup canned peaches, sliced, drained
1 cup boiling water
2 tablespoons sweetened shredded coconut

1. Arrange 4 glass custard dishes in a 9-inch square glass baking dish.

2. Pour milk in 2-pint glass dish; heat in microwave oven 3½ minutes until scalded.

3. Beat eggs until frothy; slowly add sugar and salt and beat until fluffy.

4. Gradually add milk and vanilla, stirring constantly, until well blended. Pour custard into 4 custard dishes.

5. Pour 1 cup boiling water in the square glass baking dish. Bake about 4½ minutes, turning dishes every 30 seconds until custard is barely set.

6. Remove from oven. Let stand until cool. Chill.

7. To serve, top custards with sliced peaches and sprinkle with coconut.

Makes 4 servings.

162

Virginia Floating Island

1. Pour Custard Sauce Delong into a 1-quart serving dish.

2. Beat egg whites with salt until frothy; gradually add sugar and beat until stiff.

3. Fold in vanilla.

4. Boil water in a 2-quart glass casserole.

5. Drop egg-white mixture by tablespoons to form 6 mounds into boiling water. Heat, uncovered, in microwave oven 1 minute.

6. Remove meringues with slotted spoon; drain well. Place meringues on Custard Sauce. Serve warm or chilled.

Makes 6 servings.

*Custard Sauce Delong
  (page 42)
2 egg whites
⅛ teaspoon salt
¼ cup sugar
1 teaspoon vanilla
2 cups boiling water*

Maine Tapioca Pudding

1. Combine tapioca, 3 tablespoons sugar, salt, milk, cream, and egg yolk in 1½-quart glass casserole. Mix well; let stand 5 minutes.

2. Cook, uncovered, in microwave oven 3 minutes. Stir; cook 2½ minutes longer or until mixture bubbles vigorously.

3. Remove from oven. Stir in almond flavoring; let stand 1 minute.

4. Beat egg white until frothy; add remaining 2 tablespoons sugar and beat until stiff. Fold into hot tapioca mixture. Let stand 10 minutes.

5. Serve warm or chilled.

Makes 4 servings.

*3 tablespoons minute tapioca
5 tablespoons sugar
⅛ teaspoon salt
1½ cups milk
½ cup light cream
1 egg, separated
½ teaspoon almond flavoring*

Continental Caramel Pudding

1½ cups milk
½ cup light cream
1 cup sugar
¼ cup cornstarch
⅛ teaspoon salt
1 teaspoon vanilla

1. Combine 1¼ cups milk and cream in 2-quart glass casserole; heat in microwave oven, uncovered, 5 to 7 minutes until scalding, but not boiling, stirring occasionally. Remove from oven.

2. Place sugar in 2-quart glass casserole; heat in microwave oven, uncovered, 5 minutes. Stir well; heat 4 minutes longer, stirring frequently until sugar is golden brown.

3. Slowly stir in scalded milk and cream; heat 1½ minutes, until sugar is dissolved.

4. Blend cornstarch with remaining milk; stir into hot mixture. Stir in salt. Heat 2 minutes, stirring three times. Stir in vanilla.

5. Let stand 10 minutes. Serve warm or chilled.

Makes 4 servings.

Viennese Chocolate Dessert

3 tablespoons butter
1 square unsweetened
chocolate (1 ounce)
½ cup sugar
3 eggs, separated
½ cup light cream
1½ cups soft bread crumbs
¼ cup slivered almonds
Grand Chocolate Sauce
(page 43)

1. Combine butter and chocolate in 2-quart glass baking pan; heat in microwave oven 1½ minutes, stirring once until chocolate is melted.

2. Stir in sugar; blend well.

3. Beat egg yolks and cream until fluffy; add to chocolate mixture. Cook, uncovered, 2½ minutes, stirring twice.

4. Remove from oven; let stand 5 minutes. Stir in bread crumbs and almonds; blend well.

5. Beat egg whites until stiff; fold into chocolate mixture. Bake, covered, 4 minutes, turning pan halfway twice.

6. Let stand 10 minutes. Serve warm with Grand Chocolate Sauce.

Makes 6 servings.

Old-Fashioned Salem Fluff

1. Lightly grease 8-inch square glass baking pan.

2. Beat egg whites with salt until stiff; set aside.

3. Beat egg yolks until fluffy. Add honey, graham-cracker crumbs, baking powder, walnuts, and shredded coconut; blend well.

4. Fold egg whites into egg yolk mixture. Turn into prepared baking pan. Bake in microwave oven 8 minutes, turning pan halfway twice.

5. Let stand 10 minutes. Cut into squares. Serve with Cherry Sauce Supreme.

Makes 6 servings.

3 eggs, separated
⅛ teaspoon salt
½ cup honey
1 cup graham-cracker crumbs
1 teaspoon baking powder
½ cup finely chopped walnuts
½ cup sweetened shredded coconut
Cherry Sauce Supreme (page 41)

Bulles de Rosé

1. Lightly grease 6 glass custard cups.

2. Combine flour, baking powder, and salt; mix well.

3. Combine sugar with butter; cream until fluffy. Add milk alternately with flour mixture, blending well after each addition. Fold in beaten egg whites.

4. Spoon batter into custard cups. Cover each cup securely with plastic film wrap. Bake in microwave oven 4½ minutes.

5. Remove from oven. Let stand, covered, 6 minutes.

6. Turn balls into individual dessert dishes; spoon Rosé Fruit Sauce over them.

Makes 6 servings.

1 cup flour
1 teaspoon baking powder
¼ teaspoon salt
½ cup sugar
¼ cup butter
½ cup milk
2 egg whites, stiffly beaten
Rosé Fruit Sauce (page 43)

Oriental Delight

¼ cup flour
½ teaspoon baking powder
¼ teaspoon salt
1 cup chopped dates
1 cup chopped walnuts
½ cup chopped citron
½ cup chopped pistachio nuts
2 eggs, separated
¾ cup sugar
½ teaspoon almond flavoring
Quick Vanilla Sauce (page 44)

1. Generously butter 9-inch square glass baking pan.

2. Combine flour, baking powder, and salt.

3. Combine dates, walnuts, citron, and pistachios; sprinkle flour mixture over all and blend well.

4. Beat egg yolks until fluffy; add sugar and beat until frothy and thick. Fold in date mixture with almond flavoring.

5. Beat egg whites until stiff; fold into date mixture. Turn into prepared baking pan. Bake in microwave oven 8 minutes, turning pan halfway every 2 minutes.

6. Let stand in pan until cool. Cut into squares. Serve with Quick Vanilla Sauce.

Makes 6 servings.

New England Taffy

2 cups sugar
¼ cup vinegar
¼ cup water
1 teaspoon vanilla

1. Combine sugar, vinegar, and water in 1½-quart glass casserole. Cook, uncovered, in microwave oven 6 minutes. Stir well; cook 3 minutes longer.

2. Remove from oven; test with candy thermometer to soft-crack stage, 280°F.

3. Add vanilla. Pour mixture equally onto 2 or 3 well-buttered serving platters. Let cool slightly until easy to handle.

4. With greased hands pull taffy until it turns white and is stiff. Twist pieces and cut into bite-size pieces. Wrap in waxed paper.

5. If taffy becomes too hard, heat in microwave oven to soften; cool slightly before handling.

Makes about 48 pieces.

Cheery Cherry Cobbler

1. Combine cherry pie filling and lemon juice; mix well. Turn into 1-quart shallow ungreased glass baking dish.

2. Blend margarine, sugar, flour, cinnamon, and allspice with fingers until crumbly. Work in walnuts. Sprinkle over cherry filling.

3. Heat in microwave oven 5 to 6 minutes until cobbler is bubbly.

4. Serve by spooning into individual dishes; top each with scoop of ice cream.

Makes 4 servings.

1 can cherry pie filling
  (1 pound)
1 teaspoon lemon juice
1/3 cup margarine
1/4 cup brown sugar
1 cup flour
3/4 teaspoon cinnamon
1/4 teaspoon allspice
1/2 cup chopped walnuts
1/2 pint vanilla ice cream

Strawberry Shortcake

1. Lightly grease a glass tray or glass baking sheet.

2. Combine biscuit mix and sugar; blend well with fork.

3. Stir in 3/4 cup cream; beat with fork about 20 times. Turn onto floured board; knead 10 times. Pat or roll out dough to form 6 x 9-inch rectangle. Cut into 3 x 3-inch squares; place on tray or baking sheet. Bake 4 minutes, turning sheet twice.

4. Remove from oven; split hot shortcakes. Spoon strawberries between and over layers. Top with generous serving of whipped cream.

Makes 6 servings.

2 cups biscuit mix
1/4 cup brown sugar
3/4 cup heavy cream
2 cups fresh strawberries,
  hulled, sweetened
1 1/2 cups heavy cream,
  whipped, sweetened

NOTE: If a glass tray or baking sheet is not available, use a 9 x 11-inch square of cardboard (free from wax or glue). Cover with slightly larger piece of waxed paper and arrange shortcakes or cookies on top. Bake as directed. Use fresh sheet of waxed paper for each baking.

Square Dance Cake

2 cups sugar
2 cups flour
¼ teaspoon salt
1 teaspoon baking soda
½ cup butter
½ cup margarine
1 cup water
3 tablespoons cocoa
½ cup buttermilk
2 well-beaten eggs
1 teaspoon vanilla
Trinidad Mocha Frosting
(recipe below)

1. Combine sugar, flour, salt, and baking soda; mix well and set aside.

2. Combine butter, margarine, and water in glass bowl; heat in microwave oven 2 to 3 minutes, stirring once, until butter is melted.

3. Add cocoa; heat to boiling point, about 1½ minutes. Remove from oven; let stand 1 minute.

4. Add cocoa mixture to flour mixture with buttermilk, eggs, and vanilla; beat until thoroughly blended.

5. Turn into two 12 x 8 x 2-inch glass baking pans. Bake each pan separately 8 minutes, turning pan halfway every 2 minutes.

6. Let stand 5 minutes in pan. Remove to wire rack. Frost each layer while warm, placing one layer on top of the other.

Trinidad Mocha Frosting

⅓ cup butter
3 cups confectioners' sugar
1 teaspoon cinnamon
½ teaspoon nutmeg
2 tablespoons unsweetened cocoa
1 tablespoon instant coffee
3 tablespoons hot milk
1 teaspoon brandy extract

1. Combine butter, sugar, spices, cocoa, coffee and 2 tablespoons hot milk in bowl.

2. Stir in brandy extract. Beat until mixture is smooth and fluffy, adding enough additional hot milk to make frosting of spreading consistency.

How To Bake Packaged Cake Mix

Line bottoms of two 9-inch round glass cake pans with waxed paper. Lightly butter paper. Prepare 1 package of cake mix according to package directions. Pour ½ of batter into each prepared cake pan.

Lay a sheet of waxed paper over the top of each dish.

Bake each layer separately for 5 minutes, turning the pan halfway every minute, or until the cake tester comes out clean. Let stand in pans 5 minutes. Remove to wire rack; cool thoroughly before frosting.

To bake a sheet cake: Line bottom of a 13 x 9 x 2-inch glass baking pan. Lightly butter paper. Prepare cake mix according to package directions. Turn batter into pan. Lay a sheet of waxed paper over top. Bake about 9 minutes, turning pan halfway every 2 minutes, or until cake tester comes out clean. Let stand in pan until cool. Cut in half or into squares; remove to wire rack; frost as desired.

Heirloom Fruit Cakes

1. Combine cherries, dates, citron, pineapple, orange peel, and raisins; mix well.

2. Reserve 6 pecan and 4 almond halves; combine remaining nuts and add to fruit mixture.

3. Combine flour, sugar, baking powder, and salt; mix well. Sprinkle over fruit-and-nut mixture, stirring to coat them well.

4. Add eggs and vanilla; stir until well blended.

5. Turn mixture into two 9 x 5 x 3-inch glass loaf pans. Bake each loaf separately in microwave oven 7 to 8 minutes, turning pan every 2 minutes.

6. Cool cake in pan, allowing to stand at least 1 hour.

7. Remove from pan. Wrap in foil and store in cool place. This cake may be stored for several weeks if desired.

½ pound cut-up candied cherries
¼ pound coarsely chopped dates
¼ pound chopped citron
½ pound cut-up candied pineapple
¼ pound chopped orange peel
¼ pound chopped raisins
2 cups pecan halves
1 cup almond halves
1 cup flour
½ cup sugar
1 teaspoon baking powder
¼ teaspoon salt
4 well-beaten eggs
1 teaspoon vanilla

To bake cupcakes: Place paper baking cups into glass custard cups. Prepare cake mix according to package directions. Fill cups 1/3 full with batter. Lay a sheet of waxed paper over cups. Bake in microwave oven as follows:

1 cupcake	30 seconds
2 cupcakes	1 minute
4 cupcakes	2 minutes
6 cupcakes	3 minutes

Always place cupcakes in a circle in oven when three or more are baked at one time. Do not bake more than 6 at a time.

Williamsburg Fruit Squares

½ cup butter
½ cup brown sugar
1 egg
1 cup grated raw carrots
¾ cup raisins
¼ cup chopped citron
2 teaspoons chopped candied ginger
½ cup currants
1¼ cups cake flour
1 teaspoon baking powder
½ teaspoon baking soda
½ teaspoon cinnamon
½ teaspoon nutmeg
Boston Hard Sauce (page 40)

1. Butter a 9-inch square glass baking pan.

2. Cream butter and brown sugar until fluffy; beat in egg until frothy and well blended.

3. Add carrots, raisins, citron, ginger, and currants; mix thoroughly.

4. Combine flour, baking powder, soda, cinnamon, and nutmeg; mix well. Add to carrot mixture and blend well.

5. Turn batter into prepared baking pan. Bake 11 minutes or until surface is slightly firm when touched lightly, turning pan at the end of each 2 minutes.

6. Remove from oven; let stand 15 minutes.

7. To serve, cut into squares and top with Boston Hard Sauce.

Makes 9 servings.

Winesap Apple Cake

1. Arrange apples evenly in bottom of 8-inch square glass baking pan.

2. Combine ¼ sugar, ¼ teaspoon nutmeg, and cinnamon; blend well. Sprinkle over apples.

3. Combine butter, remaining 1 cup sugar, and egg; cream until well blended and fluffy.

4. Add milk and combined baking powder and flour alternately to creamed mixture, beating well after each addition. Spread batter over apples. Bake, uncovered, in microwave oven, 10 to 12 minutes or until apples are tender, turning pan twice during baking.

5. Let stand 10 minutes. Serve warm with cream.

Makes 6 servings.

2 cups Winesap apples, pared, diced
1¼ cups sugar
¾ teaspoon nutmeg
¼ teaspoon cinnamon
1 tablespoon butter
1 egg
½ cup milk
1 teaspoon baking powder
1¼ cups flour
¾ cup heavy cream

Pennsylvania Dutch Coffeecake

1. Grease an 8-inch square pan.

2. Combine flour, baking powder and salt.

3. Beat egg until frothy; beat in sugar and butter until light and fluffy. Add milk and almond extract.

4. Beat in flour mixture until well blended. Turn ½ of batter into pan. Sprinkle evenly with ½ Brown Sugar Frosting. Repeat with remaining batter, ending with Frosting on top.

5. Heat in microwave oven 4 to 6 minutes or until cake tester comes out clean.

6. Cool partially in pan; serve warm.

1½ cups flour
2½ teaspoons baking powder
½ teaspoon salt
1 egg
¾ cup sugar
⅓ cup melted butter
½ cup milk
1 teaspoon almond extract
Brown Sugar Frosting
(page 172)

171

Brown Sugar Frosting

½ cup brown sugar
2 tablespoons soft butter
2 tablespoons flour
½ teaspoon cinnamon
¼ teaspoon allspice
¼ teaspoon nutmeg
½ cup coarsely chopped
walnuts

1. Combine all ingredients, except walnuts, in bowl; mix with fork.

2. Add walnuts; stir until blended and mixture is crumbly.

Colonial Gingerbread

1 cup flour
½ cup sugar
½ teaspoon baking soda
¼ teaspoon salt
¼ teaspoon cinnamon
½ teaspoon ground ginger
¼ cup shortening
1 well-beaten egg
1 tablespoon dark molasses
½ cup buttermilk
1 cup heavy cream, whipped

1. Combine flour, sugar, soda, salt, cinnamon, and ginger. Cut in shortening with pastry blender until mixture is crumbly; reserve ¼ cup for topping.

2. Combine remaining mixture with egg, molasses, and buttermilk; mix with fork just until blended.

3. Spread batter in 8-inch glass cake pan. Bake in microwave oven 2½ minutes, turning pan halfway once.

4. Sprinkle with reserved crumb mixture over entire surface. Bake 2½ minutes longer or until cake tester comes out clean.

5. Let stand in pan 5 minutes. Cut into wedges. Serve with whipped cream.

How to Bake Pastry Shells

1 cup flour
½ teaspoon salt
6 tablespoons shortening
3 tablespoons cold milk

1. Combine flour and salt in mixing bowl.

2. Cut in shortening with pastry blender until mixture is coarse.

3. Sprinkle with cold milk, 1 tablespoon at a time, tossing with fork. Work dough into a firm ball.

4. Roll out pastry on lightly floured board; shape into 9-inch glass pie plate. Flute edge flat with fork tines, or with fingers making a thin edge. *Do not prick shell.*

5. Cover shell with 1 layer of absorbent paper, covering edge as well. Place 8-inch glass pie plate inside the pastry shell on top of paper.

6. Bake in microwave oven 3 minutes. Remove 8-inch pie plate and paper. Bake 1½ minutes longer. Let stand 20 minutes before filling.

Hawaiian Luau Pie

1. Butter and lightly flour a 9-inch glass pie plate.

2. Beat egg whites until frothy; add sugar and continue beating until stiff. Blend in vanilla.

3. Combine graham-cracker crumbs, baking powder, salt, coconut, and macadamia nuts; mix well. Fold into egg white mixture.

4. Spread mixture in prepared pie plate. Bake in microwave oven 9 to 10 minutes, turning plate halfway every 2 minutes.

5. Let stand on wire rack until thoroughly cool.

6. Pile whipped cream lightly on surface. Chill, if desired.

4 egg whites
1 cup sugar
1 teaspoon vanilla
1 cup graham-cracker crumbs
1 teaspoon baking powder
¼ teaspoon salt
½ cup sweetened shredded coconut
½ cup chopped macadamia nuts
1 cup heavy cream, whipped

Kentucky Pecan Pie

1½ cups pecan halves
¼ cup butter
½ cup brown sugar
1 cup light corn syrup
½ teaspoon vanilla
dash nutmeg
3 eggs
1 9-inch baked pastry shell
(page 172)

1. Spread pecans in glass baking dish; heat in microwave oven 2 minutes, stirring twice. Set aside.

2. Combine butter and sugar; cream until fluffy.

3. Add corn syrup, vanilla, and nutmeg; beat well. Add eggs; beat until mixture is smooth and well blended.

4. Spread pecans evenly in pastry shell. Pour egg mixture carefully over the top. Bake 8 minutes or until set.

5. Let stand 10 minutes. Cool or chill, as desired.

Combination Cooking

Some cooked foods are better enjoyed when the surface is browned or, as in the case of meat, when it is seared or browned before cooking is completed. In this chapter you will find directions for using the conventional range, surface or oven, in combination with the microwave oven, to help you reduce the time needed in preparing your meals.

You will want to try some of these recipes and, after you have gained experience in timing and using both appliances, you will be able to use many of your favorite recipes, adjusting your cooking schedule to take advantage of this new method. Where a browner top or "crustier" appearance is desired as, for example, on a casserole, this means simply placing the finished dish under a preheated conventional broiler unit for a few minutes before serving. If you have a favorite recipe you would like to try in a microwave oven which requires a "brown" top, follow the directions as given in a similar recipe in this book, then brown under a broiler. Usually 2 or 3 minutes is all that is required.

To brown or sear steaks and other meats in a skillet on a surface range unit,

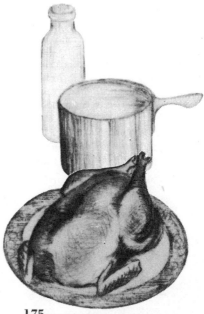

be sure both skillet and fat are hot so that only the surface of the meat will be heated, thus avoiding overcooking.

The recipes in this chapter are given as examples of what you can accomplish when using conventional and microwave cooking in combination. Foods should be thawed and be at room temperature or refrigerator temperature unless otherwise specified in the recipe.

Remember always to undertime the foods you are cooking in the microwave oven. It is just a matter of seconds or minutes if you feel you want food to be a little more done.

Meat and Poultry

Osaka Sukiyaki

*1 can bamboo shoots
(8 ounces)
1 can water chestnuts
(3½ ounces)
1 can bean sprouts (1 pound)
½ pound fresh mushrooms
2 small onions
3 stalks celery
1 pound round steak
1 tablespoon shortening
⅓ cup soy sauce
2 tablespoons sugar
1 tablespoon brown sugar
½ cup bouillon
dash Worcestershire sauce*

1. Drain bamboo shoots and water chestnuts; slice thinly.

2. Drain bean sprouts; rinse in cold water. Drain.

3. Clean mushrooms and onions; slice thinly.

4. Cut celery diagonally into thin slices.

5. *Surface Range:* Slice steak very thinly, diagonally across the grain. Heat shortening in 10-inch heat-proof ceramic or glass skillet on range. Add meat; brown very quickly, stirring with fork. Remove skillet from heat.

6. Arrange browned meat in center of skillet to form a strip. Arrange vegetables in individual piles on either side of meat.

7. *Microwave Oven:* Combine soy sauce, sugars, bouillon and Worcestershire sauce. Pour over all. Cook, uncovered, 4 minutes or until vegetables are still crisp.

8. Let stand 5 minutes.

Makes 4 servings.

Beef Stroganoff Smetana

1. Combine flour, salts, and pepper; set aside.

2. Trim any excess fat from meat. Rub both sides of meat with garlic; discard garlic.

3. Pound flour mixture into both sides of meat. Cut into strips about 1½ x 1 inch.

4. *Surface Range:* Pour oil in 10-inch heat-proof ceramic or glass skillet; heat oil. Add meat; brown on all sides.

5. *Microwave Oven:* Add onion; cook 2 minutes, stirring once.

6. Stir in soup, water, mushrooms and liquid; blend well. Cook 4 minutes, until meat is just tender.

7. Gently stir in sour cream; heat 40 seconds. Season with paprika.

8. Let stand 1 minute and serve.

Makes 4 servings.

3 tablespoons flour
1 teaspoon salt
½ teaspoon onion salt
¼ teaspoon pepper
1 pound beef tenderloin,
  sliced ¼-inch thick
1 clove garlic, halved
3 tablespoons vegetable oil
⅓ cup chopped onion
1 can cream of chicken soup
  (10½ ounces)
¼ cup water
1 can sliced mushrooms with
  liquid (4 ounces)
1 cup sour cream
paprika

Hamburger De Luxe

1. *Surface Range:* Melt shortening in 10-inch heat-proof glass or ceramic skillet on surface range unit.

2. Add beef and salt; cook over medium heat, stirring frequently until meat is browned. Pour off excess fat.

3. *Microwave Oven:* Add potatoes. Sprinkle contents of small seasoning package over potatoes. Pour boiling water over all. Cook, covered, 7 to 9 minutes or until potatoes are tender, stirring twice.

4. Let stand 5 minutes before serving.

Makes 4 servings.

1 teaspoon shortening
½ pound ground lean beef
½ teaspoon salt
1 package au gratin potatoes
  (10 ounces)
2½ cups boiling water

177

Meatballs Cathay

1 pound ground lean beef
¼ cup fine dry bread crumbs
1 tablespoon minced onion
¾ teaspoon salt
⅛ teaspoon pepper
2 cups water
1 slightly beaten egg
1 tablespoon vegetable oil
1 cup sliced celery
*2 medium green peppers,
cut into strips*
⅓ cup vinegar
⅓ cup brown sugar
1½ tablespoons soy sauce
*1½ teaspoons Worcestershire
sauce*
2 tablespoons cornstarch
*1 cup canned pineapple
chunks, drained*

1. Combine beef, bread crumbs, onion, salt, pepper, 7 tablespoons water, and egg; mix lightly with fork until well blended. Shape into 1-inch balls.

2. *Surface Range:* Heat oil in 10-inch heat-proof ceramic or glass skillet. Brown meatballs turning them over to brown evenly. Remove meatballs from skillet; set aside.

3. *Microwave Oven:* Place celery and pepper in skillet. Cook, uncovered, 4 minutes, stirring frequently.

4. Combine 1½ cups water, vinegar, sugar, soy sauce, and Worcestershire sauce in 1-quart glass casserole; stir until blended.

5. Combine cornstarch with remaining 1 tablespoon of water to form a smooth paste; stir into soy sauce mixture. Cook 5 minutes, stirring frequently.

6. Add meatballs to celery and pepper in skillet. Pour sauce over all.

7. Stir in pineapple chunks. Heat, covered, 6 minutes, stirring once.

8. Let stand 5 minutes.

9. Serve plain or over hot cooked rice or noodles.

Makes 4 servings.

French Beef Ragout

1. Combine flour, salt, and pepper.

2. Cut meat into 2-inch cubes. Coat with flour mixture.

3. *Surface Range:* Heat shortening in 10-inch heat-proof glass or ceramic skillet; add meat and brown on all sides.

4. *Microwave Oven:* Add tomato sauce, garlic, thyme, basil, wine, and vinegar. Cook, covered, 15 minutes or until beef is tender.

5. Add carrots, potatoes, celery, onions, and turnip. Cook, covered, 8 minutes longer or until vegetables are crisp-tender.

6. Let stand 6 minutes before serving.

Makes 4 servings.

1 tablespoon flour
½ teaspoon salt
⅛ teaspoon pepper
1 pound lean beef for stew
1 tablespoon vegetable oil
1 can tomato sauce (8 ounces)
1 clove garlic, minced
⅛ teaspoon thyme
⅛ teaspoon basil
¾ cup dry red wine
2 teaspoons vinegar
2 medium carrots, sliced
1 cup diced potatoes
¾ cup sliced celery
8 small whole onions
⅛ cup chopped turnip

Svenska Meatballs

1. Pour milk over bread crumbs in bowl; let stand 10 minutes.

2. Add pork, beef, egg, salt, pepper, nutmeg, Worcestershire sauce, and onion; mix lightly with fork until well blended. Shape into 1-inch balls.

3. *Surface Range:* Heat shortening in 10-inch heat-proof glass or ceramic skillet. Add meatballs; brown on all sides. Remove meatballs; set aside.

4. Stir the flour into skillet drippings until smooth and well blended. Gradually add consommé, stirring constantly.

5. *Microwave Oven:* Heat 3 minutes, stirring once until thickened and smooth.

6. Add meatballs; cook, covered, 4 minutes longer, stirring once.

7. Let stand 5 minutes before serving.

Makes 4 servings.

1 cup milk
½ cup fine dry bread crumbs
½ pound ground lean pork
½ pound ground lean beef
1 slightly beaten egg
¾ teaspoon salt
¼ teaspoon pepper
dash nutmeg
1 tablespoon Worcestershire sauce
1½ tablespoons minced onion
2 tablespoons shortening
¼ cup flour
1 cup consommé

Veal Scallopini di Napoli

¼ cup vegetable oil
1 clove garlic, halved
1 pound veal cutlet, cut into
4 thin slices
½ cup sliced onions
¼ cup sliced green onions
1 can mushrooms (6 ounces)
2 tablespoons flour
½ teaspoon salt
⅛ teaspoon pepper
water
1 can tomato sauce
(8 ounces)
dash oregano

1. *Surface Range:* Heat oil in 10-inch heat-proof glass or ceramic skillet. Add garlic; cook 2 minutes.

2. Add veal; brown on both sides. Remove veal; set aside. Discard garlic.

3. *Microwave Oven:* Add onions to skillet drippings. Drain mushrooms; reserve liquid. Add mushrooms to skillet. Cook, uncovered, 2 minutes, stirring once.

4. Stir in flour, salt, and pepper until blended. Cook 2 minutes longer.

5. Measure mushroom liquid; add enough water to make ½ cup. Combine with tomato sauce; gradually stir into flour mixture, stirring constantly until smooth. Cook 5 minutes, stirring twice.

6. Sprinkle oregano over mixture. Add browned veal. Cook, covered, 5 minutes or until meat is tender.

7. Let stand 5 minutes before serving.

Makes 4 servings.

Irish Lamb Stew

2 cups leftover or
canned gravy
1 can whole mushrooms
(8 ounces), drained
1 cup thinly sliced carrots
1 cup frozen peas
¾ pound lean lamb shoulder,
cubed
1 tablespoon flour
2 tablespoons vegetable oil
¾ teaspoon salt
¼ teaspoon pepper
2 cups hot mashed potatoes

1. Combine gravy, mushrooms, carrots, and peas in a bowl; let stand 5 minutes.

2. Roll meat in flour until coated on all sides.

3. *Surface Range:* Heat oil in 10-inch heat-proof glass or ceramic skillet. Add meat; brown on all sides.

4. *Microwave Oven:* Add gravy and vegetables. Season with salt and pepper. Mix until blended. Cook, covered, 5 minutes, stirring once.

5. Spoon mashed potatoes on top of stew. Cook, uncovered, 7 minutes or until stew is hot and bubbly.

6. Let stand 3 minutes before serving.

Makes 4 servings.

Lamb Chops Mayfair

1. Sprinkle 1 teaspoon salt and pepper over lamb chops.

2. *Surface Range:* Heat butter in skillet. Add chops and brown lightly on both sides.

3. *Microwave Oven:* Arrange chops in one layer in 2-quart glass baking pan; pour skillet drippings over the top. Cook, covered, 5 minutes.

4. Slice potatoes thinly and arrange over chops with onion slices. Season with remaining salt. Pour bouillon over all. Cook, covered, 12 to 14 minutes or until meat is tender.

5. Combine parsley, bread crumbs, and paprika; sprinkle over top. Place under broiler 1 or 2 minutes until browned.

Makes 6 servings.

1½ *teaspoons salt*
¼ *teaspoon pepper*
6 *rib lamb chops (about 2 pounds)*
2 *tablespoons butter*
1 *can whole white potatoes (1 pound)*
2 *large onions, thinly sliced*
1 *can bouillon (10½ ounces)*
2 *tablespoons minced parsley*
¼ *cup fine dry bread crumbs*
⅓ *teaspoon paprika*

Lamb Chops au Diable

1. *Surface Range:* Trim fat from chops; brown chops in shortening in 10-inch heat-proof glass or ceramic skillet, turning them once to brown on both sides.

2. *Microwave Oven:* Place butter in 1-quart glass casserole; heat 1 minute until melted.

3. Add onion; heat 1 minute, stirring once.

4. Add tomato and Worcestershire sauces, vinegar, sugar, parsley, salt, pepper, oregano, and Tabasco; stir until well blended. Pour over chops. Cook, covered, in microwave oven, 14 to 16 minutes or until meat is tender, basting with sauce occasionally.

5. Let stand 5 minutes before serving.

Makes 4 servings.

8 *rib or loin lamb chops, cut 1-inch thick*
1 *teaspoon shortening*
2 *tablespoons butter*
1 *medium onion, diced*
1 *can tomato sauce (10½ ounces)*
1 *teaspoon Worcestershire sauce*
1 *teaspoon wine vinegar*
1 *tablespoon brown sugar*
2 *tablespoons minced parsley*
½ *teaspoon salt*
⅛ *teaspoon pepper*
⅛ *teaspoon oregano*
dash Tabasco

181

Swedish Pork Chops

½ cup fine dry bread crumbs
½ teaspoon caraway seed
⅛ teaspoon pepper
1¼ teaspoons salt
1 egg
1 tablespoon water
6 pork chops, ¾-inch thick
(about 1¾ pounds)
2 tablespoons shortening
1 tablespoon flour
1 cup milk
1 cup chicken bouillon

1. Combine bread crumbs, caraway seed, pepper, ¾ teaspoon salt in shallow dish and mix well.

2. Beat egg and water in another dish until blended.

3. Roll pork chops in bread crumb mixture; dip in egg mixture, then roll in bread crumbs again.

4. *Surface Range:* Heat shortening in 10-inch heat-proof glass or ceramic skillet. Add chops and brown well on both sides. Place chops in 1 layer in shallow glass baking pan.

5. Add flour and remaining salt to skillet drippings; stir until smooth.

6. *Microwave Oven:* Gradually stir in milk and bouillon, stirring constantly until blended. Cook, uncovered, 5 minutes, stirring frequently. Pour sauce over chops. Cook, uncovered 12 minutes, turning chops over once. Let stand 5 minutes.

Makes 6 servings.

Pork Chops Aglow

1. Trim pork chops of excess fat; wipe dry with absorbent paper.

2. *Surface Range:* Sprinkle sugar in bottom of 10-inch heat-proof glass or ceramic skillet; cook over medium heat until sugar begins to brown.

3. Place pork chops in skillet; brown on both sides. Pour boiling water over chops.

4. *Microwave Oven:* Add onions, celery, and beans; cook, covered, 9 minutes, turning skillet halfway once.

5. Add cabbage; cook 2 minutes.

6. Combine cornstarch, cold water and soy sauce to make smooth paste. Stir into skillet; cook 1 minute longer.

7. Let stand 5 minutes before serving.

Makes 4 servings.

4 loin pork chops
½ teaspoon sugar
1 cup boiling water
1 large onion, sliced
½ cup sliced celery
½ pound green beans
2 cups coarsely shredded
  cabbage
1 tablespoon cornstarch
2 tablespoons cold water
3 tablespoons soy sauce

Western Franks and Beans

1. *Surface Range:* Melt butter in 10-inch heat-proof glass or ceramic skillet.

2. With paring knife lightly score frankfurters; brown in butter. Remove from skillet; set aside.

3. *Microwave Oven:* Add onion to skillet drippings; cook, uncovered, 2 minutes, stirring once.

4. Add corn syrup, sugar, mustard, Worcestershire sauce, and ginger; stir until blended. Cook 1 minute.

5. Drain lima beans, kidney beans, and garbanzos. Add to onion mixture. Cook, covered, 5 minutes.

6. Add frankfurters; cook 5 minutes longer.

7. Let stand 5 minutes before serving.

Makes 4 servings.

2 tablespoons butter
1 pound frankfurters
1 medium onion, sliced
¼ cup dark corn syrup
¼ cup brown sugar
2 teaspoons prepared mustard
1 teaspoon Worcestershire
  sauce
¼ teaspoon ground ginger
1 can lima beans (14 ounces)
1 can red kidney beans
  (1 pound, 4 ounces)
1 can garbanzos (14 ounces)

Poulet au Vin

1 tablespoon shortening
1 broiler-fryer (about 2½
to 3 pounds), cut up
1 teaspoon salt
¼ teaspoon pepper
¼ teaspoon rosemary
¼ teaspoon thyme
3 medium onions, thinly
sliced
½ cup consommé
6 tablespoons dry red wine

1. *Surface Range:* Heat shortening in 10-inch heat-proof glass or ceramic skillet.

2. Add chicken pieces; brown on all sides, turning them frequently. Drain off excess fat.

3. Season chicken with salt, pepper, rosemary, and thyme.

4. Arrange onion slices on top of chicken.

5. *Microwave Oven:* Combine consommé and wine; pour over all. Cook, uncovered, 20 to 22 minutes, turning chicken pieces several times until tender.

6. Let stand 10 minutes before serving.

Makes 4 servings.

San Simeon Barbecued Chicken

1 broiler-fryer (about 2½ to
3 pounds), cut in quarters
2 teaspoons salt
¼ teaspoon pepper
¼ cup consommé
1 cup sliced onions
½ cup tomato juice
¼ cup chili sauce
⅛ teaspoon cayenne
½ teaspoon prepared mustard
2 teaspoons Worcestershire
sauce
1 tablespoon brown sugar
1 clove garlic, minced
1 bay leaf, crumbled
6 tablespoons vinegar
1 tablespoon butter

1. Arrange chicken pieces, skin side down in 10-inch heat-proof glass or ceramic skillet. Sprinkle with 1 teaspoon salt and ⅛ teaspoon pepper.

2. *Microwave Oven:* Pour consommé over chicken; arrange onion slices on top. Cook, uncovered, 7 minutes.

3. Combine tomato juice, chili sauce, remaining salt and pepper, cayenne, mustard, Worcestershire sauce, sugar, garlic, bay leaf, vinegar, and butter in 2-pint glass bowl; stir until well blended.

4. Remove chicken from oven; let stand. Heat barbecue sauce in microwave oven 3 minutes, stirring once. Pour sauce over chicken; return to microwave oven. Cook, uncovered, 20 to 24 minutes, turning chicken occasionally and basting with sauce.

5. *Standard Oven:* Preheat conventional oven to 425°F. Place heat-proof skillet with chicken (be sure handle is also heat proof) in oven. Bake 8 to 10 minutes until chicken is nicely glazed.

Makes 4 servings.

Chicken Antoine

1. Combine flour, 1 teaspoon salt, ¼ teaspoon pepper, and cayenne; blend well. Coat chicken pieces with mixture.

2. *Surface Range:* Heat oil in 10-inch heat-proof glass or ceramic skillet. Add chicken; sauté in hot oil, turning frequently to brown on all sides. Remove chicken; set aside.

3. *Microwave Oven:* Combine onions, parsley, pimientos, garlic, saffron, rosemary, and oregano; stir into skillet. Cook 5 minutes, stirring once.

4. Add chicken to skillet. Pour tomatoes over. Sprinkle with remaining salt and pepper. Cook in microwave oven, covered, 23 to 28 minutes, depending on size of chicken, until tender.

5. Let stand 5 minutes before serving.

Makes 4 servings.

¼ cup flour
2 teaspoons salt
½ teaspoon pepper
dash cayenne
1 broiler-fryer (3 to 3½ pounds), cut up
⅓ cup vegetable oil
1 cup sliced onions
¼ cup chopped parsley
2 diced pimientos
1 clove garlic, minced
¼ teaspoon saffron
¼ teaspoon rosemary
¼ teaspoon oregano
1½ cups canned tomatoes

Chicken Calcutta

1. Combine salt, pepper, paprika, and thyme; sprinkle generously over chicken breasts.

2. *Microwave Oven:* Arrange chicken in 10-inch heat-proof glass or ceramic skillet. Cook, uncovered, 9 to 10 minutes, turning chicken over once.

3. Combine broth, onion, curry powder, and wine; blend well. Pour over chicken. Cook in microwave oven, uncovered, 16 to 18 minutes, turning every 3 minutes. About 4 minutes before cooking time is up, add mushrooms, and stir in 2 tablespoons mushroom liquid.

4. *Standard Oven:* Preheat broiler in conventional oven; broil chicken 3 inches from source of heat 3 to 4 minutes, until nicely browned.

Makes 4 to 6 servings.

1 teaspoon salt
¼ teaspoon pepper
½ teaspoon paprika
¼ teaspoon thyme
3 whole chicken breasts (about 3 pounds), split
¼ cup chicken broth
1 tablespoon minced onion
¾ teaspoon curry powder
½ cup Sauterne wine
1 can sliced mushrooms (3 ounces), reserve liquid

185

Quickie Chicken Dinner

1 broiler-fryer (3 pounds),
cut up
1 teaspoon salt
¼ teaspoon pepper
½ teaspoon paprika
¼ cup butter
3 tablespoons flour
½ cup chicken broth

1. Arrange chicken pieces in 10-inch heat-proof glass or ceramic skillet, placing large pieces in outer circle, skin side down, and small pieces in center.

2. *Microwave Oven:* Season with salt, pepper, and paprika. Cook, uncovered, 21 to 25 minutes or until chicken is tender, turning over once.

3. Remove chicken from oven; let stand.

4. Place butter in glass bowl; heat 1 minute until melted. Drizzle over chicken.

5. *Standard Oven:* Preheat broiler element and broil chicken 3 inches from source of heat, 3 to 4 minutes, turning over once, until nicely browned. Remove chicken to heated serving platter.

6. Combine flour and 3 tablespoons chicken broth; blend to a smooth paste. Stir into pan drippings until smooth.

7. *Microwave Oven:* Gradually stir in remaining chicken broth, stirring constantly; heat 3 minutes, stirring twice. Serve gravy with chicken.

Makes 4 servings.

Fish and Shellfish

Baked Perch au Gratin

1 package frozen fillets of
ocean perch (1 pound)
2 tablespoons fine cracker
crumbs
1 cup canned tomatoes
2 tablespoons chopped onion
¼ teaspoon salt
⅛ teaspoon pepper
1 tablespoon butter
¼ cup shredded Cheddar
cheese

1. *Microwave Oven:* Place unopened package of frozen fish in microwave oven and partially defrost according to directions on page 93. Remove fish from package and separate fillets.

2. Grease lightly 1-quart shallow glass baking pan. Sprinkle with cracker crumbs. Lay fillets on crumbs.

3. Combine tomatoes, onion, salt, and pepper; pour over fish. Dot with butter.

Cook, uncovered, in microwave oven 4 minutes. Turn baking dish; cook 2 minutes longer.

4. *Standard Oven:* Preheat broiler of conventional range. Sprinkle cheese over fish. Broil about 3 inches from source of heat until cheese is melted and lightly browned, about 2 to 3 minutes.

Makes 4 servings.

Classic Fried Fish

1. Place unopened package of frozen fish in microwave oven and partially defrost according to directions on page 93. Remove fish from package and separate fillets.

2. Pour oil into 1-quart shallow glass baking pan.

3. Combine egg and water and beat until blended.

4. Combine biscuit mix and ketchup and blend with fork.

5. Dip fish in egg, then in biscuit mix until well coated on both sides. Lay in baking pan, turning over once to coat both sides with oil.

6. *Microwave Oven:* Cook, uncovered, 4 minutes. Turn baking dish; cook 2 minutes longer.

7. *Standard Oven:* Preheat broiler of conventional range. Sprinkle cheese over fish. Broil 3 inches from source of heat until cheese is melted and lightly browned, about 2 to 3 minutes.

Makes 4 servings.

1 package frozen haddock
*   fillets (1 pound)*
½ cup vegetable oil
1 egg
2 tablespoons water
1 cup prepared biscuit mix
3 tablespoons ketchup
¼ cup shredded Cheddar cheese

Seafarer Oyster Pie

pastry for 2-crust 9-inch pie
1½ pints oysters, with liquid
light cream
⅓ cup butter
⅓ cup flour
1 tablespoon minced parsley
1 teaspoon salt
¼ teaspoon pepper
¾ teaspoon paprika

1. *Standard Oven:* Heat conventional oven to 450°F.

2. Divide pastry dough in 2 portions. Roll each to ⅛-inch thickness. Cut top, bottom, and 4 strips for sides, to fit 8-inch square glass baking dish. Place pastry pieces on baking sheet; prick well with fork. Bake 8 to 10 minutes until lightly browned; set aside.

3. Drain oysters; reserve liquid. Add enough cream to make 3½ cups of liquid.

4. *Microwave Oven:* Place butter in 2½-quart glass casserole; melt 1 minute.

5. Stir in flour, parsley, salt, and pepper; blend to a smooth paste. Heat 1 minute.

6. Gradually stir in cream liquid, stirring constantly until well blended and smooth. Heat 9 to 10 minutes, just to boiling point.

7. Add oysters; stir well. Heat 2 minutes just to boiling point.

8. Fit baked crust in bottom and sides of glass baking dish. Add hot oyster filling. Place crust on top. Sprinkle with paprika. Heat 1 minute. Serve at once.

Makes 6 servings.

Crabmeat Mornay

1 package frozen chopped spinach (10 ounces)
3 tablespoons butter
2 tablespoons flour
½ teaspoon salt
⅛ teaspoon pepper
1½ cups milk
½ cup light cream
1 cup grated Swiss cheese
1 tablespoon lemon juice
2 cans crabmeat (6½ ounces each), drained, flaked
¼ cup dry bread crumbs
¾ teaspoon paprika

1. *Microwave Oven:* Cook frozen spinach according to directions on page 108. Drain well. Place in 2-quart glass casserole; set aside.

2. Place butter in glass bowl; heat in microwave oven until melted, 1 minute.

3. Blend in flour, salt, and pepper until smooth. Heat 1 minute.

4. Gradually stir in milk and cream, stirring constantly until smooth. Heat 5 to 6 minutes, stirring twice, just to boiling point.

188

5. Add cheese; stir until melted. Add lemon juice and crabmeat. Pour over spinach. Cook, uncovered, 7 minutes without stirring.

6. *Standard Oven:* Preheat broiler in conventional oven. Sprinkle bread crumbs and paprika over casserole. Broil 3 inches from source of heat 2 to 3 minutes until browned.

7. Serve over toast or hot cooked rice.

Makes 6 servings.

Oahu Shrimp

1. *Microwave Oven:* Clean and devein shrimp; place in 3-quart glass casserole. Sprinkle with cayenne. Fill, barely covering shrimp with boiling water. Cook, uncovered, in microwave oven 2 minutes. Let stand 2 minutes; drain.

2. Dice shrimp; arrange in 8-inch square glass baking pan.

3. Combine mustard, sugar, Worcestershire sauce, soy sauce, butter, hot-pepper seasoning, and salt; mix thoroughly. Spread over shrimp. Sprinkle with bread crumbs. Cook, uncovered, in microwave oven 3 minutes, turning pan halfway twice.

4. *Standard Oven:* Preheat broiler in conventional range. Sprinkle cheese over pan. Broil 3 inches from source of heat 2 to 3 minutes, until cheese is melted and lightly browned.

Makes 6 servings.

3 pounds raw shrimp
dash cayenne
boiling water
2 tablespoons prepared mustard
1 teaspoon brown sugar
2 teaspoons Worcestershire sauce
1 teaspoon soy sauce
½ cup butter
3 drops liquid hot-pepper seasoning
1 teaspoon salt
½ cup buttered fresh bread crumbs
½ cup shredded sharp Cheddar cheese

Shrimp Newburg in Patty Shells

*1 package frozen patty
shells (10 ounces)
1 package frozen ready-to-
cook shrimp (12 ounces)
1 can frozen cream of shrimp
soup (10 ounces)
¼ cup light cream
1 teaspoon minced onion
½ cup grated Cheddar sheese
¼ cup Sauterne wine*

1. *Standard Oven:* Preheat conventional oven to 450°F. Bake patty shells according to package directions; set aside.

2. *Microwave Oven:* Place package of frozen shrimp in microwave oven; heat 1½ minutes until partially defrosted. Place in 2-quart glass casserole. Pour boiling water to just barely cover. Cook, uncovered, 2 minutes. Let stand 2 minutes; drain. Set aside.

3. Place frozen soup in glass bowl; heat 2 minutes until thawed. Stir. Add cream, and stir until blended. Heat 2 minutes, stirring twice.

4. Add onion and cheese; cook, uncovered, 2 minutes, until cheese is melted, stirring once.

5. Place shrimp in 1½-quart glass casserole; pour sauce over it. Stir in wine. Heat 2 minutes to just boiling point.

6. Fill warm patty shells with shrimp mixture.

Makes 6 servings.

Frozen Assets

Home food freezers, whether small compartments atop or below refrigerators or commodious separate units, have revolutionized home cooking.

They've banished tasteless leftovers and, along with them, the complaints about having the same foods warmed up several times. Now the leftovers can go into the freezer and appear days or even weeks later as something brand-new. They can be reheated in minutes in a microwave oven, and the taste be unbelievably fresh and tantalizing, because there is no drying out or reheated flavor.

Freezers also serve as bread boxes, cookie jars, and instant chefs. One need never again be caught empty-handed: Unexpected guests are not a problem any longer because a freezer contains simplified entertaining, i.e., what to feed them. The microwave oven can magically heat or cook anything from appetizers to soups to gourmet dishes to elegant desserts.

Foods remain fresh longer when they are frozen, so no more stale breads, cookies, sandwiches, cakes and pies.

191

Frozen meals also mean split-second tempting dishes, served as soon as the dinner bell rings, if you have a microwave oven. You can defrost and reheat an entire meal in minutes. No more waiting for the food to defrost, and then waiting almost an hour to heat it in the conventional oven.

Today's homemaker can cut down on the time she spends cooking by planning two meals instead of one, freezing one and having it ready at a moment's notice. This is especially attractive to the busy woman who sometimes arrives home when it's almost time to get dinner ready.

The combination of microwave oven and freezer is unbeatable in convenience, economy and time-saving planning.

Cooking Chart for Frozen Vegetables

Vegetable	Amount	Cooking Instructions	Time in Minutes
Asparagus	10 ounces	In ⅓ cup water.	6½
Beans, green, French cut	12 ounces	In ½ cup water; stir twice.	7
Beans, wax	10 ounces	In ⅔ cup water.	7½
Beans, baby lima	10 ounces	In ½ cup water.	8
Broccoli, chopped	10 ounces	In ¼ cup water; stir twice.	4½
Broccoli, spears	10 ounces	In ½ cup water.	8
Cabbage	10 ounces	In ½ cup water; add 1 teaspoon caraway seed, if desired, after 3 minutes. Stir and continue cooking.	7
Carrots	10 ounces	In ½ cup water; add ½ teaspoon sugar, if desired, after 2 minutes. Stir and continue cooking.	5½
Cauliflower	10 ounces	In ½ cup water.	4
Corn, cut	10 ounces	In ¼ cup water.	4
Corn on the cob	2 ears	Butter and season; wrap in plastic film.	3-4

192

Mixed vegetables	10 ounces	In ½ cup water.	6½
Peas	12 ounces	In ⅓ cup water.	4½
Peas and carrots	10 ounces	In ½ cup water.	5
Potatoes, french fried	9 ounces	Place on absorbent paper in paper plates.	4½
Spinach, chopped	12 ounces	Do not add any water.	4-4½
Spinach, whole	12 ounces	In 2 tablespoons water.	4½
Squash			
Acorn	1 pound	Do not add water.	4-5
Summer	12 ounces	Do not add water.	4

Use a 1½-quart glass casserole, with cover.

Place seasoning in bottom of casserole before adding vegetables and water, if any.

Heating Chart (Miscellaneous Foods)

Item	Portion	Heating Instructions	Time
Frozen Baked Foods			
Buns, hamburger and frankfurter	1 bun	Heat, uncovered, on absorbent paper, paper napkin, or serving dish	24-26 seconds
	2 buns	Same as above.	45-47 seconds
	4 buns	Same as above.	1¼ to 1½ minutes
Coffeecake	1, 10-12 ounces	Heat, uncovered, on paper plate or serving dish.	3 minutes
Danish pastries, baked	4 servings (8 ounces)	Heat, uncovered, on paper plate or serving dish.	1½-2 minutes
Dumplings, apple, baked	2 servings	Heat in serving dishes. Let stand 5 minutes before serving.	5-5½ minutes

193

Pie, fruit, baked	8-inch size	Remove from aluminum plate; place in serving plate. Temperature given is for warm pie. Let stand 5 minutes before serving.	5½-6½ minutes
Rolls, dinner, baked	2 medium	Heat, uncovered, on paper plate or serving dish.	20-25 seconds
	4 medium	Same as above.	40-50 seconds
	6 medium	Same as above; arrange in circle.	60-65 seconds

Frozen Prepared Foods

Beef roast, turkey, chicken, and other meats	4 ounces	Heat 1¼ minutes; let stand 2 minutes. Return to microwave oven and complete heating.	4-5 minutes
Chicken in gravy	1 serving	Heat 2 minutes; let stand 2 minutes. Return to microwave oven, cover, and complete heating, turning dish several times. Let stand 5 minutes before serving.	8-10 minutes
Chow mein	14 ounces	Heat 2 minutes; let stand 2 minutes. Stir. Cover and complete heating, stirring once again. Let stand 4 minutes before serving.	7-7½ minutes
Dinner, 1 meat, 2 vegetables	1 serving (10-11 ounces)	Remove from aluminum tray to dinner plate. Heat, uncovered, turning plate frequently. Let stand 2 minutes before serving.	5-6 minutes
Hamburger, cooked	1 4-ounce patty	Heat, uncovered, on serving plate. Do not overcook.	1-1½ minutes
	2 4-ounce patties	Same as above.	2-2½ minutes

Macaroni and cheese, or noodles Romanoff	8-12 ounces	Place in 1½-quart glass casserole. Cover with sheet of waxed paper. Stir halfway through cooking time. Let stand 3 to 5 minutes before serving.	4-6 minutes
Meat pies, fully baked	1 serving (8 ounces)	Remove from aluminum plate to small glass casserole. Heat, uncovered, turning dish twice.	6½-7 minutes
Potatoes, baked and stuffed	1 medium (6 ounces)	Heat, uncovered, turning several times.	3½ minutes
	2 medium (12 ounces)	Same as above.	7-7½ minutes
Soufflé, corn, unbaked	12 ounces	Heat, uncovered, turning frequently.	11-12 minutes

Leftover Foods

Room Temperature

Apple pie	1 piece (4 ounces)	Heat, uncovered, on serving plate.	15 seconds
Blueberry muffin	1 muffin	Same as above.	6 seconds
Cheese blintzes	2 blintzes	Same as above.	20 seconds
Coffee cake	1 piece (3-inch)	Place on absorbent paper in paper plate; heat, uncovered.	7 seconds
Danish pastry	1 pastry	Same as above.	6 seconds
Roll, dinner	1 roll	Heat, uncovered, on serving plate.	4
Soup	1 cup (8 ounces)	Heat, uncovered, in bowl, stirring once.	1½ minutes

Refrigerated Temperature

Cooked meat roast beef, turkey, chicken etc.	4 ounces	Heat, uncovered, on serving plate. If gravy is included or any other sauce, increase time by 1 minute.	1½-2 minutes
	8 ounces	Same as above.	2¼-3½ minutes

Hamburger, cooked	1 patty	Heat, uncovered, on serving plate. Do not overcook.	45-50 seconds
	2 patties	Same as above.	1¼-1½ minutes
Macaroni and cheese	2 cups	Place in 8-inch glass pie plate. Cover with sheet of waxed paper. Stir half-way through cooking time. Let stand 3 minutes before serving.	3-4 minutes

Freezer to Table Meals

MENU

Barbecued Meat Loaves
Baked Potatoes   **Buttered Asparagus**
Tossed Green Salad
Cherried Cream Puffs

Barbecued Meat Loaves

1½ pounds ground lean beef
⅓ cup minced onion
2 tablespoons chopped green pepper
1⅓ cups soft bread crumbs
¾ teaspoon salt
1 egg
3 tablespoons ketchup
2½ teaspoons prepared horse-radish
½ teaspoon dry mustard
½ cup milk
Snappy Barbecue Sauce (page 197)

1. Combine beef, onion, green pepper, bread crumbs, salt, egg, ketchup, horse-radish, mustard, and milk. Toss lightly with fork and blend thoroughly.

2. Shape into 6 small, individual loaves, about 3½ x 2 inches. Place 3 loaves in each of two 1½-quart shallow glass baking pans, to form a circle.

3. Cook, uncovered, in microwave oven 6 minutes, 1 baking pan at a time, turning halfway once, and basting with barbecue sauce. Cook 6 to 8 minutes longer, turning pan twice and basting with sauce.

4. Remove from oven. Let stand until cool.

196

To Freeze

Wrap each individual loaf in moisture-proof material; label and date. Freeze.

To Serve

Unwrap; place frozen meat loaf in glass baking pan. Heat, uncovered, in microwave oven 2 minutes. Remove from oven; let stand 4 minutes. Return to oven; heat 5 to 5½ minutes longer, turning pan twice. Serve with Snappy Barbecue Sauce.

1 meat loaf	7-7½ minutes
2 meat loaves	9-9½ minutes
4 meat loaves	11-12½ minutes
6 meat loaves	13 to 15 minutes

Makes 6 servings.

Snappy Barbecue Sauce

1. Combine ketchup, Worcestershire and soy sauces, cayenne, chili powder, and vinegar in 1½-quart glass casserole; blend well.

2. Combine bouillon, sugar, garlic, and onion in bowl; stir until blended. Let stand 10 minutes.

3. Pour bouillon mixture into ketchup mixture and stir. Cook, uncovered, in microwave oven 3 minutes, stirring once. Cover; cook 20 minutes longer, stirring several times during cooking period.

4. Remove garlic. Let stand until cool.

Makes 1 quart.

2¼ cups ketchup
2 tablespoons Worcestershire sauce
½ teaspoon soy sauce
¾ teaspoon cayenne
¾ teaspoon chili powder
½ cup tarragon vinegar
1 cup bouillon
¾ cup sugar
6 cloves garlic
2 tablespoons minced onion

To Freeze

Pour cooled sauce in freezer container; cover and freeze.

To Serve

Dip freezer container in hot water for a few seconds; dump frozen block of sauce in 2-quart glass casserole. Heat in microwave oven 2 minutes. Remove from oven; break up sauce with fork and let stand 4 minutes. Return to oven and heat 3 to 5 minutes until bubbly.

Cherried Cream Puffs

½ cup butter
¼ teaspoon salt
1 cup water
1 cup flour
4 eggs
1 quart vanilla ice cream
Cherry Sauce Supreme
(page 41)

1. *Standard Oven:* Heat conventional oven to 375° F.

2. Place butter, salt, and water in saucepan; bring to boil and stir until butter is melted.

3. Add flour all at once. Beat vigorously until mixture is thick and smooth and leaves the sides of pan. Remove from heat; continue beating until slightly cool, about 1 minute.

4. Add eggs, one at a time, beating well after each addition until mixture is smooth and blended.

5. Drop into mounds, about 2 inches apart, on greased baking sheets. Bake in standard oven 55 minutes to 1 hour until golden brown.

6. Cool cream puffs thoroughly; then split crosswise. Remove all of the inside of the puffs, leaving a shell.

7. Fill cream puff shells with ice cream. Wrap and freeze immediately.

Makes 18 puffs.

To Freeze

Place cream puffs in cartons, 2 in each carton. Seal and label. Or wrap individually in moistureproof material; label. Freeze.

To Serve

Unwrap completely or remove cream puffs from freezer cartons. Place on individual serving plates. Let stand at room temperature 30 minutes. Serve with Cherry Sauce Supreme.

MENU

Hors d'Oeuvre Marat
Stuffed Peppers with Tomato Sauce
Vegetable Medley   Gelatin Salad
Refrigerator Cheesecake

Hors d'Oeuvre Marat

1. Trim crusts from bread. Flatten slices well with rolling pin. Spread one side of each slice with butter; refrigerate 10 minutes.

2. *Standard Oven:* Preheat broiler for 10 minutes. Spread unbuttered side of each bread slice with some of the filling. Fold over to form triangle; slice each in half. Secure with wooden pick.

3. Place on ungreased baking sheet; broil 1 to 2 minutes or until lightly toasted. Cool.

4. Remove wooden picks.

Makes 28 appetizers.

14 slices thin-sliced white bread
soft butter
Favorite Fillings (recipe below)

To Freeze

Place hors d'oeuvres in freezer cartons in convenient numbers for serving. Seal and freeze.

To Serve

Place frozen hors d'oeuvres, seven or eight, in a circle in a paper plate or glass serving dish. Heat in microwave oven 1½ to 2 minutes until thoroughly hot. Serve at once.

Favorite Fillings

Cheesy Delight

Combine ½ cup coarsely chopped cooked ham, ¼ cup grated Cheddar cheese, 2 tablespoons chopped celery, dash dry mustard, and 2 tablespoons mayonnaise.

199

Goldenrod Filling

Combine 3 tablespoons grated Cheddar cheese, 4 coarsely chopped hard-cooked egg yolks, 4 crisp bacon slices, crumbled, 2 tablespoons chopped celery, 3 tablespoons mayonnaise, and 1 teaspoon prepared mustard.

Snappy Spread

Combine 1 cup coarsely chopped canned luncheon meat, ½ cup chopped sweet pickle, and ¼ cup mayonnaise.

Stuffed Peppers with Tomato Sauce

4 medium green peppers
1 cup cooked rice
1 cup coarsely chopped,
cooked roast beef
1 can tomato sauce
(8 ounces)
½ teaspoon salt
⅛ teaspoon pepper
½ teaspoon basil
1 tablespoon minced onion
¼ cup minced celery
1 can tomato sauce with
mushrooms (8 ounces)

1. Wash peppers, remove seeds and membrane. Parboil in microwave oven, in salted, boiling water, 2 minutes; drain.

2. Combine rice, chopped beef, tomato sauce, salt, pepper, basil, onion, and celery; mix thoroughly.

3. Fill peppers with stuffing. Place in 8-inch square glass baking pan. Cook in microwave oven, uncovered, 10 to 11 minutes.

4. Let stand 5 minutes before serving. Serve with tomato sauce with mushrooms, heated in glass bowl in microwave oven 4 minutes until bubbly.

Makes 4 servings.

To Freeze

Place cool stuffed peppers in freezer cartons; seal and freeze.

To Serve

Place frozen peppers in 8-inch glass baking pan; heat, uncovered, in microwave oven 18 to 20 minutes until hot. Serve with tomato sauce with mushrooms as directed in recipe above.

Vegetable Medley

1. Place butter in glass bowl; heat in microwave oven 30 seconds until melted.

2. Add cereal and curry powder; stir. Cook 2 minutes; set aside.

3. Cook vegetables in microwave oven as directed on page 108. Combine with celery soup and ¾ cup of cereal mixture. Turn into buttered 1-quart glass casserole.

4. Top with remaining cereal. Cook in microwave oven 5 to 6 minutes turning casserole halfway once.

Makes 4 servings.

1½ tablespoons butter
1¼ cups crushed shredded wheat
¼ teaspoon curry powder
1 package mixed vegetables (10 ounces)
1 can cream of celery soup (10½ ounces)

Refrigerator Cheesecake

1. Combine wafer crumbs, ¼ cup sugar, and butter in 9-inch glass pie plate; blend well. Press evenly over sides and bottom of pie plate. Bake in microwave oven 1¾ minutes, turning plate halfway 4 times.

2. Remove from oven; let stand until cool.

3. Combine cream cheese, eggs, remaining sugar, and almond flavoring in mixing bowl; beat until smooth and creamy. Spoon filling into cooled crumb crust.

4. Cut squares of chocolate in four pieces and place in glass bowl; heat in microwave oven 2 minutes until melted. Drizzle over cake filling. Sprinkle with nutmeg. Bake 4 minutes, turning plate halfway after each minute.

5. Let stand until cool. Chill in refrigerator before serving.

Makes 8 servings.

1 cup crushed vanilla-wafer crumbs
¾ cup sugar
¼ cup soft butter
4 packages cream cheese (3 ounces each), at room temperature
2 eggs
1 teaspoon almond flavoring
2 squares semi-sweet chocolate (1 ounce each)
¼ teaspoon nutmeg

MENU

Alabama Chicken Legs
Rajah Polenta   Buttered Peas
Lettuce Wedges with French Dressing
Devil's Food Cupcakes

Alabama Chicken Legs

¼ cup flour
½ teaspoon salt
¼ teaspoon paprika
dash cayenne
4 chicken legs
⅓ cup shortening
¼ cup water

1. Combine flour, salt, paprika, and cayenne; mix well. Roll chicken legs in mixture until well coated.

2. Heat shortening in 10-inch heat-proof glass or ceramic skillet over surface range unit. Add chicken legs and sauté, turning legs over to brown evenly and thoroughly.

3. Add water to skillet. Cook, covered, in microwave oven 10 to 12 minutes or until tender.

4. Let stand until cool.

Makes 4 servings.

To Freeze

Wrap cooled chicken legs in moisture-proof material. Freeze.

To Serve

Unwrap and place unthawed chicken legs in shallow glass baking pan, thick side outward. Heat in microwave oven 1½ minutes. Let stand 4 minutes. Heat 2 minutes longer.

Rajah Polenta

1. *Microwave Oven:* Combine cornmeal, water, and salt in 1½-quart glass casserole; stir well until blended. Cook, uncovered, in microwave oven 5 minutes, stirring once. Cook 3 minutes longer. Stir well.

2. Remove from oven. Add cheese, paprika, and cayenne; blend well. Heat 1 minute.

3. Let stand, covered, 5 minutes. Pour mixture into 8-inch square baking pan. Cover with plastic film. Chill in refrigerator 3 hours or overnight.

4. *Standard Range:* When ready to serve, cut Polenta into slices. Coat each slice lightly with flour. Sauté slowly in hot bacon drippings in skillet on surface range unit, turning over once.

5. Serve with Rajah Sauce.

Makes 4 servings.

½ cup white cornmeal
2 cups water
¾ teaspoon salt
½ cup grated Cheddar cheese
⅛ teaspoon paprika
dash cayenne
flour
3 tablespoons bacon
  drippings
Rajah Sauce (page 38)

Devil's Food Cupcakes

1. Combine shortening, salt, soda, and vanilla in mixing bowl. Beat until mixture is creamy.

2. Gradually add sugar, beating until light and fluffy.

3. Add egg, beat until well blended. Add chocolate; blend thoroughly.

4. Add flour alternately with milk, beating after each addition.

5. Place large-size paper baking cups into 6-ounce glass custard cups. Fill cups ⅓ full of batter. Lay a sheet of waxed paper over the tops.

6. Place 6 cupcakes in a circle in microwave oven; bake 3 minutes. Repeat with remaining 6 cupcakes.

7. Let stand until cool.

Makes 12 cupcakes.

¼ cup shortening
½ teaspoon salt
½ teaspoon baking soda
½ teaspoon vanilla
⅔ cup sugar
1 egg
1½ squares unsweetened
  chocolate (1 ounce each),
  melted, cooled
1 cup cake flour
½ cup milk

To Freeze

Wrap each cupcake in plastic film. Place in freezer cartons in convenient numbers for serving; freeze.

To Serve

Remove cupcakes from carton but do not remove plastic film. Let stand at room temperature 25 minutes. Or remove plastic film and heat in microwave oven 30 seconds for each cupcake.

MENU

Continental Onion Soup
Chicken a la King on Waffles
Celery Sticks   Carrot Curls
Mincemeat Triangles

Continental Onion Soup

¼ *cup butter*
3 cups thinly sliced onions
¾ *teaspoon salt*
⅛ *teaspoon pepper*
6 cups warm water
¼ *teaspoon bottled brown seasoning sauce*
5 beef bouillon cubes

1. Place butter in 3-quart glass casserole; heat in microwave oven 1 minute until melted.

2. Add onions; cook 3 minutes, stirring once. Sprinkle with salt and pepper.

3. Add water, seasoning sauce, and bouillon cubes. Cook, uncovered, 30 minutes stirring every 10 minutes.

4. Let stand until cool.

Makes 6 servings.

To Freeze

Pour cooled soup into three 1-pint containers, leaving 1-inch head space. Close containers; freeze.

To Serve

Thaw soup just enough to remove block from container by running container under hot water for a minute. Place block in glass casserole. Heat in microwave oven 2 minutes; remove from oven, let stand 5 minutes, stirring soup to break up frozen pieces. Return to oven; heat 4 to 6 minutes to boiling point.

Place a 2-inch round of toasted French bread on soup in each bowl. Sprinkle with Parmesan cheese. If desired, heat each bowl for 30 seconds in microwave oven.

Chicken a la King on Waffles

1. Place butter in 2-quart glass casserole; heat in microwave oven 1 minute until melted.

2. Add mushrooms and green pepper; cook 2 minutes, stirring once.

3. Add flour; stir until blended. Gradually add milk, stirring constantly until smooth. Season with salt and pepper. Cook, uncovered, 4 minutes, stirring occasionally.

4. Add cream, pimiento, and chicken. Cook, uncovered, 8 to 10 minutes until bubbly, stirring twice.

5. Gradually add 3 tablespoons of the heated sauce to egg yolk, stirring until blended; return to casserole and mix thoroughly. Cook 2 minutes until thickened.

6. Let stand until cool.

Makes 6 servings.

1 tablespoon butter
½ cup sliced canned
  mushrooms, drained
¼ cup chopped green pepper
3 tablespoons flour
1½ cups milk
1 teaspoon salt
⅛ teaspoon white pepper
¼ cup light cream
2 tablespoons chopped
  pimiento
1½ cups cooked, diced
  chicken
1 slightly beaten egg yolk
Crispy Waffles (page 206)

To Freeze

Pour Chicken a la King mixture into two 1-pint containers. Seal; freeze.

To Serve

Remove block of frozen Chicken a la King from container by running container under hot water for a minute. Place in 1½-quart glass casserole. Heat in microwave oven 2 minutes. Remove from oven; break up block in several pieces when thawed. Return to oven; heat to serving temperature, 5 to 7 minutes. Stir well to completely blend before serving.

Serve spooned over waffles.

Crispy Waffles

2 cups cake flour
1 tablespoon baking powder
1 teaspoon salt
2 tablespoons sugar
3 eggs, separated
1½ cups milk
½ cup vegetable oil

1. Combine flour, baking powder, salt, and sugar; mix well.

2. Beat egg yolks until frothy. Add milk and oil; blend well. Add to flour mixture and stir until blended.

3. Beat egg whites until stiff; fold into batter.

4. Bake in hot waffle iron to desired crispness. Cool thoroughly.

Makes 6 servings.

To Freeze

Divide waffles into quarters, or leave whole, as desired. Place piece of moisture-proof material between layers. Wrap securely and freeze.

To Serve

Unwrap waffle pieces. Heat each piece in microwave oven 30 seconds.

Mincemeat Triangles

pastry for 9-inch 2-crust pie
¾ cup mincemeat
milk
Elegant Lemon Sauce
(page 42)

1. *Standard Oven:* Heat conventional oven to 425° F.

2. Roll pastry into a 15-inch square, 1/8 inch thick. Cut into nine 5-inch squares.

3. Place 1½ tablespoons mincemeat on

206

each square. Moisten edges of pastry with water; fold over half of squares, forming a triangle. Seal edges tightly.

4. Place turnovers on baking sheet. Prick top of each one with fork to allow steam to escape. Brush top with milk. Bake 20 minutes in conventional oven.

5. Let stand until cool.

Makes 10 turnovers.

To Freeze

Place in cartons in convenient numbers for serving. Seal and freeze.

To Serve

Unwrap and place in paper plate, 5 in a circle; heat in microwave oven 2½ minutes. Serve warm with Elegant Lemon Sauce.

MENU

Glazed Ham Loaf
Potatoes Louis   Cole Slaw
Orange Sherbet
Vanilla Wafers
Glazed Ham Loaf

1. Combine ham, pork, cracker crumbs, onion, eggs, salt, milk, cream, and parsley; mix lightly but thoroughly.

2. Turn mixture into a 9 x 5 x 3-inch glass loaf pan.

3. Combine sugar, vinegar, and dry mustard in glass bowl; heat in microwave oven 1 minute, stirring once.

4. Pour sugar mixture over loaf, spreading it evenly. Bake in microwave oven 14 minutes, turning pan several times during cooking period.

5. Let stand until cool.

Makes 4 servings.

1 pound ground lean cooked ham
1 pound ground lean pork
¾ cup coarsely rolled cracker crumbs
3 tablespoons chopped onion
2 well-beaten eggs
¾ teaspoon salt
½ cup milk
½ cup light cream
1 tablespoon chopped parsley
¼ cup brown sugar
¼ cup cider vinegar
1½ teaspoons dry mustard

207

Wrap cooled ham loaf in moistureproof material. Freeze.

To Serve

Place frozen ham loaf in shallow glass baking pan. Heat in microwave oven 2½ minutes, turning once. Remove from oven; let stand 5 minutes. Return to oven. Heat 5 to 7 minutes until heated through.

Potatoes Louis

4 uniform baking potatoes
(about 7 ounces each)
2 tablespoons butter
¾ cup sour cream
1 slightly beaten egg
½ teaspoon salt
⅛ teaspoon celery salt
¼ teaspoon pepper
6 crisp bacon slices,
crumbled
paprika

1. Scrub potatoes well. Prick each potato all the way through with metal skewer, ice pick, or large fork in several places.

2. Arrange potatoes in a circle on 1 layer of absorbent paper, about 1 inch apart, in microwave oven. Bake 14 to 16 minutes, turning potatoes halfway through cooking time.

3. Remove from oven; let stand 4 minutes.

4. Cut a thin slice through skin to form an oval on top of each potato. Carefully scoop out potato from skins, leaving shells intact.

5. Combine potatoes with butter, sour cream, egg, salt, celery salt, and pepper; mash, then whip mixture until light and fluffy. Stir in crumbled bacon.

6. Lightly spoon potato mixture back into shells.

7. Sprinkle with paprika. Let stand until thoroughly cooled.

Makes 4 servings.

To Freeze

Wrap each potato in moistureproof material. Freeze.

To Serve

Unwrap frozen potatoes. Place in a circle on 1 layer absorbent paper in microwave oven. Bake 10 to 13 minutes until thoroughly heated.

Vanilla Wafers

1. Combine shortening and sugar; cream until light and fluffy. Blend in vanilla.

2. Add 2 eggs, 1 at a time, beating well after each addition. Add milk; blend thoroughly.

3. Combine flour, baking powder, and salt; mix well. Add to shortening mixture and blend thoroughly. Chill in refrigerator 2 hours or until dough is firm.

4. Roll dough on lightly floured board to 1/8-inch thickness. Cut with 2-inch cookie cutter.

5. Cut a 9 x 11-inch piece of cardboard. Cover top with slightly larger piece of waxed paper. Arrange 8 cookies on waxed paper, 1-inch apart in a square design.

6. Beat remaining egg well; brush tops of cookies. Sprinkle some cookies with coconut and others with chopped walnuts. Bake in microwave oven 1¾ minutes, turning cardboard halfway after the first 45 seconds.

7. Remove cookies from oven; let stand 1 minute. Remove from waxed paper with spatula. Discard used paper.

8. Continue baking remaining cookies, using a fresh sheet of waxed paper on the cardboard for each baking, until all ingredients are used.

Makes about 5 dozen cookies.

½ cup shortening
1 cup sugar
1½ teaspoons vanilla
3 eggs
2 tablespoons milk
2¾ cups flour
2 teaspoons baking powder
1 teaspoon salt
shredded sweetened coconut
chopped walnuts

To Freeze

Cool cookies thoroughly at room temperature. Package in freezer cartons in convenient serving amounts. Seal; freeze.

To Serve

Remove cookies from carton; place on serving plate. Let stand at room temperature 10 minutes before serving.

MENU

Spaghetti with Sauce Romano
Spinach, Lettuce, and Cucumber Salad
with Italian Dressing
Old-Country Yeast Rolls
Spumoni Cake

Spaghetti with Sauce Romano

2 tablespoons olive oil
½ pound ground lean beef
1 large onion, finely chopped
3 tablespoons minced parsley
1 clove garlic, minced
¼ cup chopped celery
¼ cup chopped green pepper
1 can tomatoes (1 pound)
1 can tomato paste (6 ounces)
¾ teaspoon salt
¼ teaspoon pepper
¼ teaspoon thyme
¼ teaspoon oregano
⅛ teaspoon nutmeg
½ cup bouillon
1 package spaghetti (8 ounces)
Parmesan cheese, grated

1. Heat oil in 10-inch heat-proof glass or ceramic skillet on surface range unit.

2. Add meat; cook until browned, stirring frequently with fork to crumble meat.

3. Add onion, parsley, garlic, celery, and green pepper. Cook, covered, in microwave oven 5 minutes.

4. Add tomatoes, tomato paste, salt, pepper, thyme, oregano, and nutmeg; stir until well blended. Cook, covered, in microwave oven 5 minutes.

5. Add bouillon; stir. Continue cooking 15 minutes longer, stirring frequently.

6. Let sauce stand, covered, 10 minutes before serving over cooked spaghetti.

7. Cook spaghetti according to directions on page 124.

8. Spoon sauce over spaghetti; sprinkle with Parmesan cheese.

Makes 4 servings.

To Freeze Spaghetti Sauce

Cool thoroughly. Pour into two 1-pint

containers leaving 1-inch head space. Cover; freeze.

Or, pour sauce into ice trays with dividers. Freeze. Transfer cubes to freezer containers.

To Serve

Remove block of frozen sauce from container by running container under hot water for a minute. Place in 1½-quart glass casserole. Heat in microwave oven 2 minutes. Remove from oven; break up block in several pieces when thawed. Return to oven; heat to serving temperature 5 to 7 minutes. Stir well to completely blend before serving.

Or, place as many frozen cubes as needed in 1½-quart glass casserole. Heat in microwave oven 5 to 9 minutes, depending on quantity, stirring frequently until thawed and blended.

Old Country Yeast Rolls

1. Combine hot milk, salt, shortening, molasses, sugar, and oats; mix well. Cool to lukewarm.

2. Dissolve yeast in lukewarm water. Add softened yeast, egg, and 1 cup flour to milk mixture; beat until smooth.

3. Gradually add enough remaining flour to make a soft but firm dough, stirring until well mixed. Turn onto lightly floured board. Knead about 10 minutes until elastic.

4. Place dough in greased bowl; turn over once and cover with damp towel. Let rise in warm place until doubled.

5. Punch down. Shape dough into balls of a size to half fill greased muffin pans. Cover; let rise until doubled.

6. Heat conventional oven to 400°F. Bake rolls 15 to 18 minutes until nicely browned.

Makes 18 rolls.

¾ cup milk, scalded
1½ teaspoons salt
2 tablespoons shortening
2 tablespoons molasses
2 tablespoons brown sugar
1 cup quick-cooking rolled oats, uncooked
1 package active dry yeast
⅓ cup warm water
1 well-beaten egg
2¾ to 3 cups flour

To Freeze

Wrap in moistureproof material being careful not to crush them. Freeze until hard. Stack into containers in convenient serving numbers. Store in freezer.

To Serve

Unwrap frozen rolls. Place on serving dish or on paper napkin. Heat in microwave oven:

2 rolls	20-25 seconds
4 rolls	40-50 seconds
6 rolls	60-70 seconds

Or, let stand at room temperature until thawed. Heat in microwave oven:

2 rolls	10-12 seconds
4 rolls	18-20 seconds
6 rolls	24-26 seconds

Spumoni Cake

*1 package yellow cake mix
(about 18 ounces)
1 quart spumoni ice cream* or
*Neapolitan ice cream
Cardinal Sauce (page 41)*

1. Prepare cake mix and bake in two 8- or 9-inch layers according to directions on page 168.

2. Let stand on wire racks until thoroughly cooled.

3. Split cake layers. Working quickly spread ice cream evenly between layers of cake, ending with 4 layers of cake and 3 layers of ice cream.

Makes 14 servings.

To Freeze

Wrap in moistureproof material and store in freezer until needed.

To Serve

Place wrapped cake on cake rack; let stand at room temperature until thawed enough to cut into wedge-shaped pieces.

Place pieces on individual serving plates. Let stand just until cake is completely thawed but ice cream is still firm, about 10 to 15 minutes. Spoon Cardinal Sauce over each piece.

NOTE: If you wish to serve only a portion of the cake, place wrapped cake on wire rack; let stand at room temperature until thawed enough to cut into desired servings and place these on plates. Wrap and refreeze unused portion of cake.

MENU

Pea Soup Lexington
Southern Pork Savory
Florida Salad Bowl   Hot Garlic Bread
Tropical Banana Cake

Pea Soup Lexington

1. Combine peas, minced green onions, salt, nutmeg, and water in 2-quart glass casserole. Cook, covered, in microwave oven 10 minutes, stirring to break up frozen peas after 5 minutes. Let stand 10 minutes.

2. Press mixture and liquid through fine sieve until smooth. Return to casserole.

3. Stir in chicken broth. Cook, covered, 5 minutes to boiling point.

4. Stir in cream; let stand 4 minutes before serving.

5. To serve, ladle in individual bowls and sprinkle with chopped green onions.

Makes 8 servings.

2 packages frozen green peas
(10 ounces each)
½ cup minced green onions
½ teaspoon salt
dash nutmeg
¾ cup water
1 can chicken broth
(10½ ounces)
½ cup heavy cream
2 tablespoons chopped green
onions

213

Southern Pork Savory

1 pound lean pork, cut into
1-inch cubes
1 teaspoon salt
¼ teaspoon pepper
1 teaspoon shortening
1 cup water
1 cup sliced carrots
⅓ cup flour
1 cup sour cream
1¼ cups diced potatoes
1 teaspoon chopped onion
¾ cup green lima beans

1. Sprinkle pork with ½ teaspoon salt and ⅛ teaspoon pepper. Brown in shortening in 10-inch heat-proof glass or ceramic skillet, turning cubes over to brown evenly.

2. Add water. Cook, covered, in microwave oven 12 minutes. Add carrots; cook 5 minutes longer, stirring once.

3. Combine flour with sour cream; beat until smooth. Stir into meat mixture.

4. Add potatoes, onion, and lima beans. Cook, covered, 9 to 10 minutes longer or until vegetables are just tender.

5. Let stand 5 minutes before serving.

Makes 8 servings.

To Freeze

Spoon into 2 freezer containers leaving 1-inch head space, after being thoroughly cooled. Seal; store in freezer.

To Serve

Remove block of frozen meat mixture from container by running container under hot water for a minute. Place in 1½-quart glass casserole. Heat in microwave oven 2 minutes. Remove from oven; break up block in several pieces when thawed. Return to oven; heat to serving temperature, 5 to 7 minutes. Stir well to completely blend before serving.

214

Florida Salad Bowl

1. Wash cauliflower thoroughly in running cold water; drain. Separate into flowerets and slice thin lengthwise.

2. Wash lettuce; break into bite-size pieces.

3. Combine cauliflower, lettuce, onion, sliced olives, blue cheese, and radishes in salad bowl; toss lightly to mix. Chill 30 minutes.

4. Just before serving; add dressing to salad; toss thoroughly.

5. Serve garnished with parsley.

Makes 8 servings.

2 packages frozen cauliflower (10 ounces each), thawed
1 small head lettuce
⅔ cup thinly sliced Bermuda onion
½ cup sliced stuffed green olives
½ cup crumbled blue cheese
6 radishes, thinly sliced
⅔ cup French dressing
8 parsley sprigs

Hot Garlic Bread

1. Cut loaf of bread in half crosswise. Make diagonal cuts in each half at 1-inch intervals, taking care not to cut through bottom.

2. Combine butter, garlic, cheese, oregano, marjoram, pepper, and paprika; mix until well blended. Spread mixture between bread slices.

3. Place each half of bread on paper plate or serving plate. Heat each half separately in microwave oven 1½ minutes or until butter is melted and bread is hot.

Makes 8 servings.

1 loaf French bread
½ cup soft butter
1 clove garlic, minced
3 tablespoons grated Parmesan cheese
½ teaspoon oregano
½ teaspoon marjoram
¼ teaspoon pepper
¼ teaspoon paprika

215

Tropical Banana Cake

½ cup butter
1½ cups sugar
3 eggs, separated
1¼ cups mashed bananas
1 teaspoon baking soda
½ cup sour cream
2 cups flour
dash mace
1 teaspoon vanilla
Brazilian Chocolate Frosting
(page 217)

1. Cream butter; gradually add sugar and cream until fluffy.

2. Beat egg yolks; add to butter mixture and beat until blended. Add bananas; blend.

3. Combine baking soda with sour cream. Combine flour with mace. Add sour cream and flour mixtures alternately to banana mixture, blending thoroughly.

4. Beat egg whites until stiff; fold in vanilla. Fold into batter. Turn into two 8-inch round glass cake pans. Bake each layer separately for 6 minutes in microwave oven, turning pan halfway every 1½ minutes.

5. Let stand until thoroughly cooled. If used immediately, frost with Brazilian Chocolate Frosting.

Makes 8 servings.

To Freeze

Remove cooled cake layers from pan; wrap in moistureproof material; store in freezer.

To Serve

Place each frozen cake layer on serving plate; heat in microwave oven 2 to 2½ minutes.

Or, let stand at room temperature until thawed. Frost as desired.

Brazilian Chocolate Frosting

1. Beat egg until light and fluffy. Gradually add sugar; continue beating until well blended.

2. Melt chocolate in paper wrappers in microwave oven 1½ to 2 minutes.

3. Combine mace and salt.

4. Place butter in glass bowl; heat in microwave oven 30 seconds until barely softened.

5. Combine sugar mixture, chocolate, mace, salt, and butter; beat until smooth and of desired spreading consistency. Stir in vanilla.

1 egg
2 cups confectioners' sugar
2 squares unsweetened chocolate (1 ounce each)
¼ teaspoon salt
dash mace
⅓ cup butter
1 teaspoon vanilla

217

General Cooking Guide

Glossary

Bake	To cook by dry heat.
Baste	To moisten food with sauce, liquid, or melted fat to add flavor.
Blend	To combine two or more ingredients thoroughly.
Boil	To cook in liquid at boiling temperature. Boiling point is reached when bubbles are formed on the surface of the liquid.
Braise	To brown food in small amount of hot fat, then cook, covered, over simmering heat.
Broil	To cook under direct heat.
Coat	To cover surface of foods evenly with mixture of flour and seasonings; or with bread crumbs; or with sugar, crumbs and nuts. Also, to dip in beaten egg or milk and then in seasoned flour or crumbs.
Combine	To mix together all ingredients.
Cool	To let stand at room temperature until no longer warm.
Cut in	To use a pastry blender or two knives to distribute solid shortening through dry ingredients.

Dot	To scatter small bits of butter or other ingredients over surface of food.
Dust	To sprinkle lightly with flour or sugar.
Fold in	To combine light ingredients (such as stiff-beaten egg whites or whipped cream) into batter, using a gentle motion with rubber scraper.
Glaze	To coat with barbecue sauce, syrup, or jelly during cooking.
Heat	In microwave energy cooking, it is used to denote either cooking or heating of food.
Knead	To work dough by stretching it with the hands, folding it over, and pressing until it is elastic and smooth.
Marinate	To let food stand in acid mixture, usually oil, vinegar, and seasonings.
Parboil	To boil in liquid until partially cooked.
Poach	To cook in simmering liquid.
Roast	To cook by dry heat.
Sauté	To cook in small amount of hot fat.
Scald	To heat liquid just below the boiling point.
Sear	To brown surface of meat quickly by intense heat.
Toss	To stir and lightly lift ingredients, usually with a fork.

Substitutions of Ingredients

Baking powder	1 teaspoon = ¼ teaspoon baking soda plus ½ teaspoon cream of tartar.
Chocolate	1 square (1 ounce) = 3 tablespoons cocoa plus 1½ teaspoons shortening.
Cornstarch	1 tablespoon = 2 tablespoons flour.
Cream light heavy	 1 cup = ⅞ cup milk plus 3 tablespoons butter. 1 cup = ¾ cup milk plus ⅓ cup butter. (Cannot be used for whipping.)
Egg	1 average-size egg = 2 egg yolks plus 1 tablespoon water, if used in baking recipe with flour; or 2 egg yolks, if used in puddings and custards.
Flour all-purpose cake	 1 tablespoon = ½ tablespoon cornstarch or 2 teaspoons quick-cooking tapioca. (Use only for thickening sauces and gravies.) 1 cup = 1 cup all-purpose flour less 2 tablespoons.
Herbs	1 tablespoon chopped fresh herbs = ½ teaspoon dried herbs.
Milk sour	1 cup = ½ cup evaporated milk plus ½ cup water; or 1 cup reconstituted nonfat dry milk plus 2 tablespoons butter. 1 cup = 1 cup sweet milk plus 1 tablespoon lemon juice or white vinegar.

Table of Equivalent Amounts

Bread crumbs	1 slice fresh bread = ¾ cup soft crumbs. 3 to 4 slices oven-dried bread = 1 cup fine bread crumbs.
Butter	½ cup = 8 tablespoons or 1 stick. 2 cups = 1 pound or 4 sticks.
Cheese cottage cream Cheddar Parmesan	 ½ pound = 1 cup. 3 ounces = 6 tablespoons. ¼ pound = 1 cup, shredded. ¼ pound = 1 cup, grated.
Coconut	3½-ounce can, flaked = 1⅓ cups.

221

Cornmeal	1 cup, uncooked = 4 cups cooked.
Crackers	
graham	15 crackers = 1 cup fine crumbs.
Cream	1 cup heavy cream = 2 cups whipped.
Dates	8 ounces pitted = 1¼ cups, cut up.
Eggs	5 medium = 1 cup 8 medium egg whites = 1 cup. 12 to 14 medium egg yolks = 1 cup.
Flour	
all-purpose	1 pound = 4 cups.
Gelatin	1 envelope = 1 tablespoon.
Lemon	1 medium = 2 to 3 tablespoons juice, or 1 tablespoon grated peel.
Macaroni	8 ounces = 4 cups cooked.
Milk	
sweetened, con- densed	15½-ounce can = 1⅓ cups.
evaporated	8-ounce can = ¾ cup. 14½-ounce can = 1⅔ cups.
Noodles	8 ounces = 4 cups cooked.
Nuts	
almonds	5 ounces = 1 cup.
peanuts	5 ounces = 1 cup.
pecans, chopped	4¼ ounces = 1 cup.
walnuts, chopped	4½ ounces = 1 cup.
Onion	1 medium = ½ cup chopped.
Orange	1 medium = ⅓ to ½ cup juice, or 2 to 3 tablespoons grated peel.
Potatoes	
white	1 pound raw, unpared = 2 cups mashed.
sweet	1 pound = 3 medium potatoes.
Raisins	1 pound = 3 cups.
Rice	
converted, un- cooked	1 cup = 4 cups cooked
precooked, un- cooked	1 cup = 2 cups cooked.
regular, white	1 cup uncooked = 3 cups cooked.

Shortening	1 pound = 2½ cups.
Spaghetti	8 ounces = 4 cups cooked.

Sugar
brown	1 pound = 2¼ cups.
confectioners'	1 pound = 4 cups unsifted or 4½ cups sifted.
granulated	1 pound = 2½ cups.

Syrup
corn	1 pint light or dark = 2 cups.
honey	1 pound = 1½ cups.
maple	12 ounces = 1½ cups.
molasses	1 pound light or dark = 1⅓ cups.

Tomatoes	1 pound = 3 medium

Weights and Measures

Dash	less than ⅛ teaspoon
1 tablespoon	3 teaspoons
4 tablespoons	¼ cup
5⅓ tablespoons	⅓ cup
8 tablespoons	½ cup
12 tablespoons	¾ cup
16 tablespoons	1 cup
1 fluid ounce	2 tablespoons
8 fluid ounces	1 cup or ½ pint
16 fluid ounces	2 cups or 1 pint
2 pints (4 cups)	1 quart
4 quarts	1 gallon
8 quarts	1 peck (dry)
4 pecks	1 bushel
16 ounces	1 pound

Bibliography

Apgar, J., Cox, N., Downey, I., and Fenton, F. "Electronic Cooking of Pork." *Journal of the American Dietetic Association* 35 (December, 1959).

Belderock, B., and Root, M.J.M. "Das Auftauen tiefgrefrorener Backwaren durch Mikrowellen." *Brot und Gebäck* 11 (1967) 221-224.

Campbell, C.L., Proctor, B.E., and Lin, T.Y. "Microwave vs. Conventional Cooking." *Journal of the American Dietetic Association* 34 (1958) 365-370.

Cathcart, W.H., and Parker, J.J. "Defrosting Frozen Foods by High-Frequency Heat." *Food Research* 11 (1946) 341-344.

Causey, K., and Fenton, F. "Effect of Reheating on Palatability, Nutritive Value, and Bacterial Count of Frozen Cooked Foods." *Journal of the American Dietetic Association* 27 (1951) 390, 491.

Copson, D.A. "Microwave Baking." *Western Baker* 22, No. 3 (1954).

———. "Microwave Cooking." *Forum Review* 4, No. 11-12 (1962).

———. *Microwave Heating in Freeze-Drying, Electronic Ovens, and Other Applications.* Avi Publishing (Westport, Connecticut: 1962).

———. Neumann, B.R., and Brody, A.L. "High Frequency Cooking, Browning Methods in Microwave Cooking." *Journal of Agricultural Food and Chemistry* 3 (1955) 424-427.

Curran, J.E. "Microwave 'Cookers' in Industry." *New Scientist* (May) 450-452.

Davis, D., and Boyd, C.A. "Family Meal Management and Microwave Cooking." *Microwave Energy Application Newsletter* 3, (1970) 3-5.

Decareau, R.V. "Utilization of Microwave Cookery in Meat Processing." *Microwave Energy Application Newsletter*, 1 (1970) 3-4.

———. *ABC's of Microwave Cooking.* Decareau (Amherst, New Hampshire: 1970).

De Loor, G.P., and Meijboom, F.W. "The Dielectric Constant of Food and Other Materials with High Water Contents at Microwave Frequencies." *Journal of Food Technology* 1 (1966) 313-322.

Fenton, F. "Research on Electronic Cooking." *Journal of Home Economics* 49 (1957) 709-712.

Fetty, H.J. *Microwave Baking of Partially Baked Products.* Proceedings of the 42nd Annual Meeting of the American Society of Bakery (1966) 144-152.

Gintzton, E.L. *Microwave Measurements.* McGraw-Hill (New York: 1957).

Hafner, T. "Die Behandlung von Lebensmitteln mit Hochfrequenz." *Brown Boveri Mitteil* 55 (1968) 124-129.

Hendler, E., and Hardy, J.D. "Heating of Human Skin by Microwave Radiation." *Digest of the 1961 International Conference on Medical Electronics* (New York: 1961) 192.

Huxsoll, C.C., and Morgan, A.I., Jr. "Microwaves for Quick-Cooking Rice." *Cereal Science Today* 13 (1968) 203-206.

Kylen, A.M., Charles, V.R., McGrath, B.H., Schleter, J.M., West, L.C., and Van Duyne, F.O. "Microwave Cooking of Vegetables." *Journal of the American Dietetic Association* 39 (1961) 321-326.

Levine, A.S. "Packaging for Microwave Cooking." *Microwave Energy Applications Newsletter* 3 (1970) 3-6, 7.

McConnel, D.R. "Microwave Ovens—Revolution in Cooking." Part 1: "Operating Principles and Design." *Electronics World* (August, 1970).

———. "Microwave Ovens—Revolution in Cooking." Part 2: "Radiation and Safety." *Electronics World* (August, 1970).

Meisel, N. "The Thawing of Food Products by Microwaves." *Industries Alimentaires et Agricoles* 86 (1969) 1251-1257.

Muchmore, R.B. *Essentials of Microwaves.* John Wiley and Sons (New York: 1952).

Park, E.R. "We Cook with Microwaves." *Journal of the American Hospital Association* (January 16, 1957).

Pence, J.W., Stanridge, N.N., and Copley, M.J. "Effect of Temperature and Relative Humidity on the Rate of Defrosting of Commercial Bread." *Food Technology* 10 (1956) 492-495.

Pietermaat, F. "Le Chauffage par Micro-Ondes." *Inter-Electronique* 23 (1968) 50-63.

Pollack, G.A. and Foin, L.C. "Comparative Heating Efficiencies of a Microwave Oven and a Conventional Electric Oven." *Food Technology* 14 (1960) 454-457.

Proctor, B.E., and Goldblith, S.A. "Radar Energy for Rapid Food Cooking and Blanching and Its Effect on Vitamin Content." *Food Technology* 2 (1948) 95-104.

Smith, D.P. "Precooking to Avoid Warmed-Over Flavor." *Broiler Industry* (January, 1968).

——, Nicolls, J.W., Moore, R.I., and Gundaker, W.E. *Laboratory Testing and Evaluation of Microwave Ovens.* Report No. BRH/ DEP 70-25, Bureau of Radiological Health, U.S. Dept. of Health, Education and Welfare (October, 1970).

Thomas, M.H., Brenner, S.B., Eaton, A., and Craig, V. "Effect of Electronic Cooking on Nutritive Value of Foods." *Journal of the American Dietetic Association* 25 (1949) 39-44.

Van Dyke, D., Wang, D.I.C., and Goldblith, S.A. "Dielectric Loss Factor of Reconstituted Ground Beef: The Effect of Chemical Composition." *Food Technology* 23 (1969) 84-86.

Van Zante, H.J. "Some Effects of Microwave Cooking Power Upon Certain Basic Food Components." *Microwave Energy Applications Newsletter* 1, 3-9.

Index